$25.^{00}$

The 4300 4-8-2's

Southern Pacific's

The 4300 4-8-2's

Robert J. Church

Revised Edition

Signature Press
Wilton, California

Mt-Class Locomotives

Published by Signature Press
11508 Green Road
Wilton, CA 95693

Publishers Cataloging-in Publication
(prepared by Quality Books Inc.)

Church, Robert J.
  The 4300 4-8-2's : Southern Pacific's Mt-class locomotives /
Robert J. Church. – Rev. ed.
  p. cm.
  Includes bibliographical references and index.
  ISBN 0-9633791-4-3

  1. Locomotives–United States. 2. Southern Pacific Railroad
Company. I. Title.

TJ606.3.S6C48 1996   625.2'61'0973
                                QBI96-20070

Library of Congress Catalog Card No. 96-67272

First Edition published by
Central Valley Railroad Publications
1980

Revised Edition, 1996
Printed in the United States of America.

Acknowledgements

THIS REVISED EDITION of my book about Southern Pacific's Mountain-type engines represents both expansion and also enhancement of the original. An undertaking to provide a detailed and comprehensive study of the 4300's could not have been accomplished without the help of many individuals. Official records that cover the many aspects pertaining to these locomotives have long since been disposed of, but fortunately much material has ended up in the collections of SP historians. It is to the generosity of these individuals that I owe a great deal of gratitude. They have taken the time to answer questions, look up material and share records and photos for use herein.

For assistance from the Southern Pacific's General Offices at San Francisco a special acknowledgment must go to George Kraus, Bureau of News, and Steve Peery, Mechanical Department. Thanks also to Guy L. Dunscomb, who has unselfishly made available the excellent photos from his collection, both his own and those taken by the late D.L. Joslyn, for no work could be considered complete without Joslyn's official company photos; to Al Phelps, retired SP employee, who over the years chronicled the steam locomotives' use, both by camera and written log, and whose collection and recollections on operations are invaluable; and to Wilbur Whittaker for the use of many photos from his fine camera work.

The following are sincerely noted and thanked for their contribution of photos: Harold B. Miller, Jeff Winslow, Jim Ady, Jim Orem, Frank Gillenwaters, Doug Richter, Stan Kistler, Alan Aske, John Illman, and Art Laidlaw, and to Guy C. Denechaud and his father R.G. Denechaud for the use of the color photo of "52." To the following, for their assistance with data: Joe Strapac, Dennis Beeghly, Ed Yungling, and Don Yungling, and for graphic assistance, Anatoly B. Ray. Thank you to Herb Joiner for his fine darkroom work, and a very sincere thank you to railroad artist Ernie Towler whose beautiful rendition of steam in action adorns the Contents page.

As with any project such as this, as soon as it is printed, much additional material comes forth. There are numerous individuals to whom I am grateful for contacting me with further information, photos, or both. The additional color photos now included have been provided by the splendid camera work of noted photographic historians Stan Kistler, Guy Dunscomb, and Jack Whitmeyer. Other slides came from the collections of Donald Duke and R.R. Wallin.

Over these past years, Arnold Menke has not only amassed the most thorough documentation of SP tender history and use, but also has collected a vast number of locomotive negatives. Those who have examined books on the history of SP steam power will have seen Arnold's presentations on tender history. Arnold was gracious enough to take the time to completely upgrade the section he wrote for the first edition of this book. The information herein is now much more comprehensive. Many additional black and white photos in this edition are from his collection and his darkroom work. He also suggested numerous improvements and additions to the first edition.

I consider it a privilege to have the opportunity to use photography from the camera of Richard Steinheimer. There is no doubt of his universal recognition as a true artist and of his willingness to share his work so others might enjoy it.

Technologies change, and these book projects are now completely done on the computer. My longtime friend and now publishing business partner, Anthony Thompson, is sincerely thanked for his editing, typography, and layout work.

The greatest benefit in gathering historical material and putting it into book form is the people who are met in the process. True friendships of long standing are cultivated, and this, alone, makes it all worthwhile.

Most of all, I must express a sincere thank you to my family, my children David, Dan and Eileen, who "left Dad alone" so he could spend endless hours in the hobby room, and to my wife, Jeanne, who devoted many hours proofreading copy of a subject she unselfishly tolerates but does not share the avid interest.

Robert J. Church

Ernie Towler

Contents

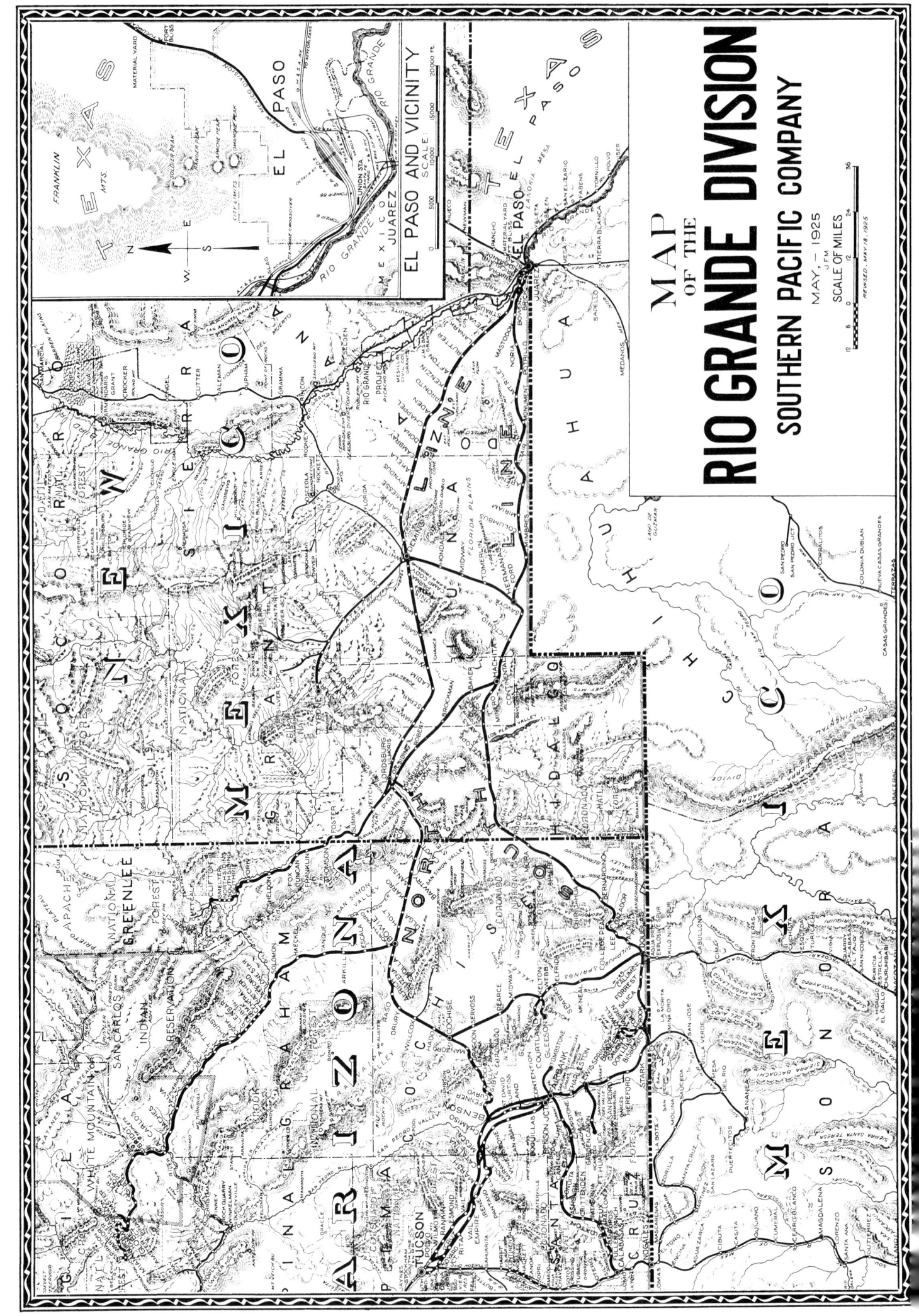

MAP
OF THE
RIO GRANDE DIVISION
SOUTHERN PACIFIC COMPANY

MAY, — 1925
JFM
SCALE OF MILES

REVISED MAY 18, 1925

EL PASO AND VICINITY
SCALE:
5000   10000   15000   20000 FT.

Developing The Locomotive

The new and the old. Built in 1925, the 4-8-2 had a tractive effort of 67,660 lbs. The 1863 built C.P. Huntington had a tractive effort of 3,510 lbs. Guy Dunscomb collection.

IN THE EARLY 1920s the Southern Pacific embarked upon a program that was to revolutionize traditional standards of steam locomotive operations, when the SP took the initiative in developing extended locomotive runs. In 1921, the operating department had placed in service powerful, Baldwin-built P-8 class 4-6-2's to haul such name trains as the *Overland Limited*, the *Pacific Limited* and the *Fast Mail* across the Overland Route between Ogden, Utah, and Sparks, Nevada, a distance of 536 miles. This run set a record for long-distance locomotive operations at the time. General practice of most roads in that era was to change motive power at major division points. On the Salt Lake Division the Espee had previously changed passenger power at Carlin, Nevada.

The new 4-6-2's could haul 11 heavyweight passenger cars, weighing a total of 875 tons, over a 1.5 percent grade, thus eliminating many helper districts on this route. These "Pacifics" averaged better than 10,000 miles per month. The success in increasing locomotive capacity and reducing the number of locomotive changes on long-distance runs was mainly due to the SP's adoption of a longer 30-inch cylinder stroke on these superheated passenger locomotives. This new design kept down cylinder clearances and gained more economical steam consumption.

Experts agreed that the P-8 4-6-2's set an exceptionally high mark in general ability to handle passenger trains. The booster-equipped trailing truck allowed for smooth starting by eliminating jerks in taking up slack. The use of a superheater and feedwater heater allowed new records in economy. New spring rigging design and equalization gave the 4-6-2's excellent stability and prompted W. L. Hack, Salt Lake Division Superintendent, to state, "These locomotives stand straight and ride straight with no nosing motion," so that "gauge and line trouble with the track disappears, even under severe weather conditions."

In continuing the program of increasing locomotive performance for longer runs and higher capacity, the Espee during this same period also began rejuvenating some of its older passenger power. Four 4-4-2

Classic examples of turn of the century passenger power. Right photo, T. Taber photo at Phoenix, 1928. Both from A. Menke collection.

Class A-3's were modernized, two at Sacramento Shops in 1927, becoming 2nd 3000 and 3001, and two at Los Angeles Shops in 1928, becoming 2nd 3002 and 3003. These engines became Class A-6. With the addition of a superheater, feedwater heater, auxiliary booster, Walschaert valve gear and other economy appliances, the tractive power of these A-6's was increased 46.6 percent over their previous ability. Eventually 47 Pacific Lines 4-4-2's were extensively rebuilt, 7 with boosters.

Some of the first 4-4-2 rebuilds were assigned to the *Daylight Limiteds*, between San Francisco and Los Angeles on the Coast Route. With a small, 10,000-gallon tank of water, these more efficient engines could run from Los Angeles to San Luis Obispo without an intermediate water stop, a distance of 230 miles. Some early 4-6-2's, nine from Class P-1 and one from Class P-3, were rebuilt with appliances similar to those applied to the A-6's. These rebuilt engines were designated Class P-4, and they too proved the efficiency gained with the use of the new technology now available in locomotive concept and design.

With success and statistics tucked under their belts, officials at San Francisco began looking for a way to speed up passenger operations on the Sunset Route between Los Angeles and El Paso. Traffic increases caused longer trains, which overtaxed the limits of the big Pacifics, and schedules had to include time for numerous helper attachments and cutoffs. Orders went to the General Superintendent of Motive Power, George McCormick, to begin the task of designing a new locomotive. It would have to be capable of hauling 14 heavyweight Pullman cars on a straight track up a grade of 26 feet per mile (0.5 percent) at a speed of 50 miles per hour, or a freight train of 75 cars at a speed of 10 miles per hour on the same grade. Maximum tractive power achieved had to be within weight limits, and ample boiler capacity was required for a design featuring long cylinder stroke on an engine that would be

Class A-6 1928 rebuild with booster, feedwater heater, and Walschaert valve gear. 1930, Al Phelps photo.

Class P-1 4-6-2, built in Oct., 1906. Some of this class were rebuilt to Class P-4 in 1924. Shown here on No. 234, at Niles Station, Dec. 11, 1938. Wilbur Whittaker photo.

A-6 rebuild No. 3000 in "Daylight" colors when used on "Sacramento Daylight" connecting at Lathrop with the "San Joaquin Daylight". Al Phelps photo.

Class P-4 1924 rebuild, showing Walschaert valve gear, Worthington feedwater heater, booster trailing truck. Sacramento, Sept., 1936, Al Phelps photo.

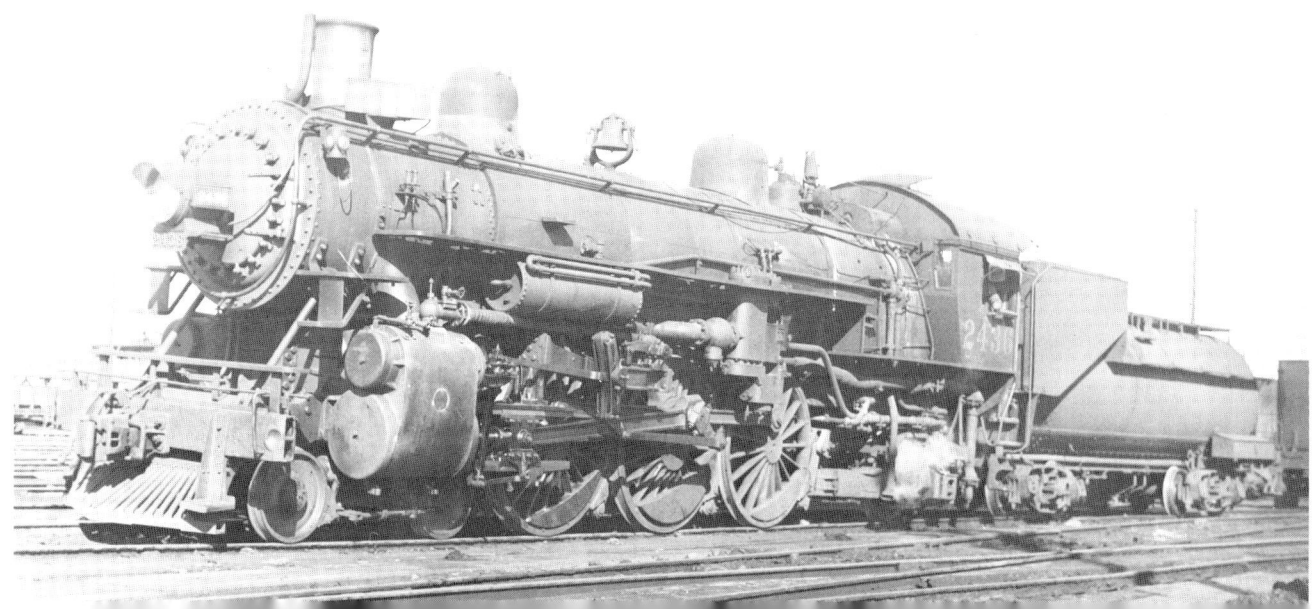

Examples of the Baldwin-built P-8 class 4-6-2's of 1921. Technology and experience gained in designing these big engines were incorporated in the new 4-8-2 wheel arrangement. Upper – No. 2470 at Stockton, July 15, 1951. Lower – Train No. 7, the *Shasta*, at Berkeley, Sept. 28, 1940. Both photos, W.C. Whittaker.

working up heavy grades and on long sustained runs.

A brief look at the characteristics of the Sunset Route's territory over which these new locomotives were being designed to operate will provide an idea of what Mr. McCormick's office had to contend with. Grades of 2 percent existed from Colton to Beaumont going east, and Indio to Beaumont going west. Also, from Tucson to Dragoon going east, grades were 1.5 percent. Previously, through trains were hauled over

these districts of heaviest grades by 2-8-2 type locomotives, and by 4-6-0 and 4-6-2 locomotives where the grades were lighter. With trains varying from 8 to 12 cars, the time card called for schedules for the *Sunset Limited* of 24 miles per hour from Colton to Beaumont, and 26 miles per hour from Indio to Beaumont. From Tucson to Dragoon the schedule was about 30 miles per hour. Most of the remaining portions of the line consisted of grades of approximately 1 percent,

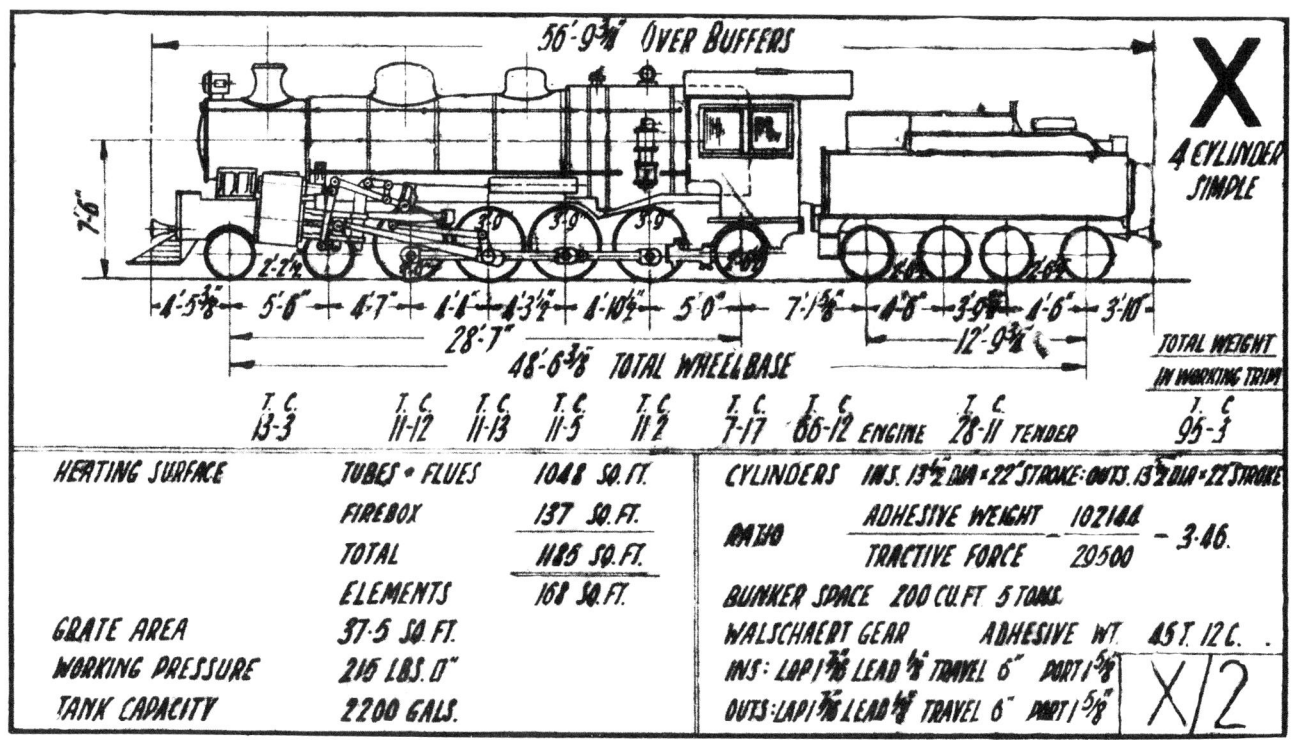

New Zealand Railways Class X locomotive diagram

theschedule varying from 38 to 42 mph. The new locomotives were to have high sustained steam capacity and power to bring the maximum and minimum operating speeds nearer the average.

To meet these requirements the Motive Power Department decided to utilize a totally new wheel arrangement, the 4-8-2 or "Mountain" type locomotive. This locomotive type had first been designed and built as such by the New Zealand Government Railways in 1908 as Class X four-cylinder compounds. The first United States railroad to adopt the 4-8-2 was the Chesapeake and Ohio when, in 1911, they had the American Locomotive Company build a group of low-drivered, powerful engines to operate in the Blue Ridge and Allegheny Mountains on slow, heavy trains. The term "Mountain type" was coined and stuck, as it was used by all the other railroads save one, the New

York Central. They felt the designation "Mountain" wasn't fitting for locomotives used on their fast water level route, so their 4-8-2's were named "Mohawks." By the early 1930s over 2000 4-8-2's were in service on the railroads across the United States.

The general design and specifications for SP's engines were worked up under both George McCormick and Frank E. Russell, the Assistant Mechanical Engineer. The contract to build 10 engines went to American Locomotive Co. in early 1923. Final details were worked out at Schenectady by the builders and the top men from Espee's mechanical department. Construction began promptly to complete the engines by year's end. The railroad wanted to place them in service as soon as possible, in keeping with its general policy and company pride to provide passenger patrons with the fastest and most modern service available. ∎

Diagram and general specifications for the new SP Mt-1 Class 4-8-2

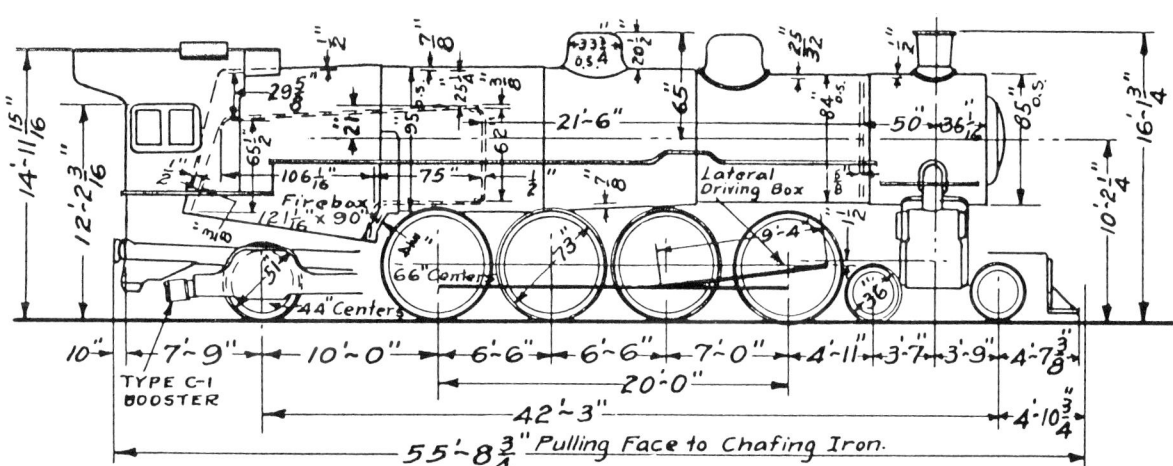

NEARING COMPLETION AT SACRAMENTO

From the Builders

THE SOUTHERN PACIFIC placed into service a total of 83 locomotives of the 4-8-2 wheel arrangement between 1923 and 1930. The engines were numbered in the 4300 series, were classified Mt-1 through Mt-5, and all were assigned to the Pacific Lines, the lines west of El Paso. The Texas and New Orleans trackage, east of El Paso, was designated the Atlantic Lines of the SP; those lines never owned a 4-8-2. Of the five classes of Mt's, only the first two were delivered from a builder, in both cases the American Locomotive Company. Classes Mt-3, 4, and 5, were all built by the Southern Pacific at its huge Sacramento General Shops.

In subsequent chapters covering each class, it is noted that all classes were very similar except for the Mt-2 class. Those six locomotives were actually designed and built for the El Paso & Southwestern by Alco, and as will be seen, did not have the lines of standard Espee power. The Southern Pacific acquired control of the EP & SW on November 8, 1924, and with the company came 146 steam locomotives, six of which were the newly-ordered 4-8-2's, so the SP, having already taken delivery of ten Mt-1 engines in December, 1923, and 18 more in May, 1924, designated the EP & SW 4-8-2's as Class Mt-2. Since the Espee already had plans to enlarge its own 4-8-2 fleet, the Mt-2's were given numbers in the 4300 series, but high in the sequence, Nos. 4385-4390. This enabled the Southern Pacific to number in consecutive order any 4-8-2's built in the future along its own design. This chapter covers those engines built for or by the SP. The Mt-2 class differences are discussed in a later chapter.

By the mid-1920s, locomotive theory, design, and engineering had become very refined, incorporating economies in fuel and water consumption, and economies of wear and maintenance, both to the locomotive and the rails and roadbed. Not only did the new locomotive of that period incorporate all the modern appliances that the individual railroad deemed necessary on an engine that met its individual operating demands, but also the latest technology in materials was applied. This often meant using materials of high tensile strength to minimize the weight of appropriate parts.

The foundation for the locomotive was the **frame**. The Mt-1's came from Alco with built-up frames using high-grade cast steel which permitted considerable weight reduction. The side frames and crossties were separate castings and were welded and bolted to the frame castings. The rear section was a Commonwealth Steel Co. cradle casting. To facilitate repairs to the booster, the front end of the cradle was designed so that the trailing truck could be dropped down without moving the truck back. Two 16 x 12 inch driver **brake cylinders** were secured to the main frames just back of the steam cylinders and were placed horizontally to relieve the frames of unnecessary stresses due to braking.

The locomotives built by the Espee at Sacramento either had similar built-up frames or a one-piece **cast steel engine bed**. The cast engine bed was first developed by the Commonwealth Steel Co. of Granite City, Ill., after many years of studying the technique required to cast such a huge piece. The SP was one of the first railroads to use this new type of engine bed. The first five engine beds purchased by the Espee were designed and cast by Commonwealth and were subject to approval of the railroad. They were applied to the first five Mt-3's being built at Sacramento. Many but not all of the Mt-3, 4, and 5's had cast engine beds. Sacramento Shops could handle casting of cylinders, and individual components of a built-up frame, but did not tackle the immense job of casting a one-piece engine bed.

Builders plate Mt-1 4326

Builders plate Mt-4 4361

Locomotive 4344 in overhead crane slings, ready to meet its running gear. Note that this is a built-up frame employing cast side frames (see drawing below) which has been given a whiting test.

These engine beds were, at the time, among the largest and most intricate steel castings ever produced. They were 52 ft. 2½ inches long and 4 ft. 3½ inches in maximum depth. A complete bed, including the rear cradle and pedestal binders, weighed 40,000 lbs. The cast steel used in the beds contained 0.18 percent (by weight) carbon, and 0.73 percent manganese, a typical low-carbon cast steel. The mold and coring were set up right in the floor of the foundry using synthetic sand, and molten steel was poured from a ladle containing nearly 50 tons of steel, requiring almost 11 minutes to pour a complete engine bed. The machining of such enormous castings required specially designed planers and slotters that were brought to the frame.

On the Mt-3 class, the front bumper and cylinders were separate castings, but by 1927, the technique had been improved to cast the cylinders and front bumper integral with the frame. These were used on those Mt-4 and 5 engines that were built with cast engine beds.

The **cylinders** of these engines were 28 inches in diameter with a stroke length of 30 inches. The long stroke was the result of the earlier data gained in tests of the P-8 locomotives that had proved so outstanding. Longer stroke had been used on freight locomotives, but its use on passenger engines was a departure from the standard practice at that time. The cylinders fol-

Cast steel side frame for Mt-1 class 4-8-2 locomotive.

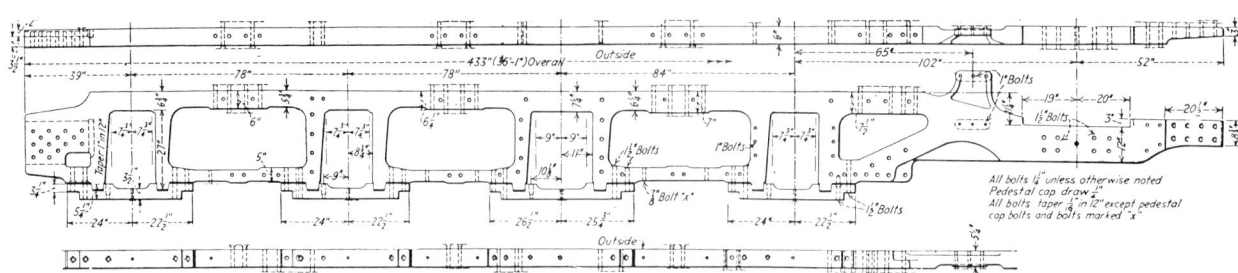

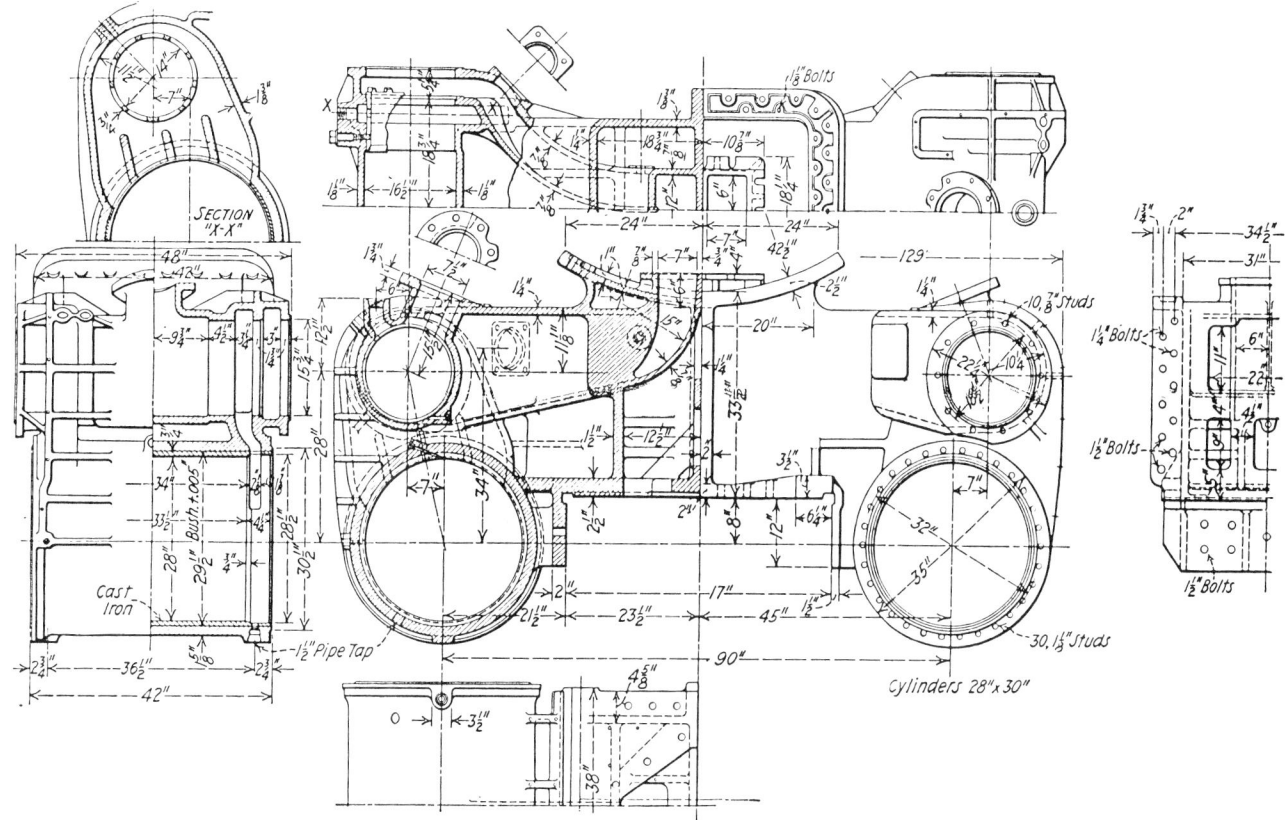

Cylinders, 28 in. x 30 in., for Southern Pacific.

lowed the American Locomotive Company's light design, except the SP had worked out a modification wherein the exhaust passages were enlarged considerably above those which were in general use. The size of the opening at the top of the saddle was 7 by 12 inches, thus providing unrestricted exhaust passage up the exhaust nozzle. The rapid escape of the exhaust reduced the back pressure of steam against the pistons. The cylinders also provided for outside steam pipes and connections for superheated steam to the booster and exhaust steam to the feedwater heater.

The **exhaust stand** was secured by twelve 1⅛-inch tee-head bolts. The cylinder exhaust passages were extended 4 inches above the cylinder saddle and were provided with a 1⅛-inch flange, well reinforced with ribs extending down to and adjoining the cylinder saddle. This construction eliminated troubles experienced in maintaining a tight joint, the absence of which interfered with the draft of the locomotive.

The **exhaust nozzle** was 8 inches in diameter and was fitted with a ½-inch square iron cross-split set 45 degrees diagonally. The cross-split created a swirling effect of the exhaust as it blasted through the nozzle and this caused the exhaust to fill the stack completely, which then provided the draft by producing a vacuum. This draft pulled the fire fumes to the smokebox.

The **smokestack** was a new Southern Pacific design.

It consisted of four iron castings assembled so that the extension of the stack in the smokebox could easily be removed for inspection of the front end of the boiler. The casting forming the extension, which was most subject to wear and pitting, could be replaced with very little trouble and without disturbing the alignment of the smokestack and base. The castings forming the lower portion of the extension were designed so that the height of the bell above the exhaust nozzle could be increased or decreased to give the best draft condition.

One of the outstanding features of this locomotive was that the design accomplished increased tractive effort without increasing the stresses set up in the track and roadbed. This was done in part by equipping the engine with a constant-resistance **centering device** to minimize lateral motion on straight track, and fitting the forward pair of drivers with the Franklin **lateral motion device**. The Franklin device accounted for the extra space between the front and main drivers. When entering a curve the front driver would move to the side when the lateral pressure reached so many pounds. This would allow the second drivers to absorb some of the stress, reducing flange wear on both the lead truck and front drivers, and reducing track stresses and lessening the danger of derailment.

The **journal bearings** were unusually large for the driving and truck axles. The main bearing was 13

Left — Springpad lubricator fitted to bottom of journal box. Glass bullseye to check oil level can be seen. Cellar was held in position by latches, easily slid out to refill.
Below — Tire safety clips

inches in diameter and 13 inches long, while the other drive wheel bearings were 11 inches in diameter and 13 inches long. These large bearings increased the life of the wearing parts and lessened the chance of a hot journal during the long distances these locomotives ran. The frame brace crossties forming the extended pedestals for the main driving boxes were of high-grade cast steel, well secured to the pedestals, and tied together top and bottom by supplementary pedestal binders. This increased rigidity of the pedestals prevented journal bearings and axles from wearing conically.

When the engines were built the bearings were lubricated by conventional waste packing and mechanical lubricators. In 1939 SP developed and patented **spring-pad lubricators** and these were installed on all engine and tender journals of the Mt classes. No Mt's had roller bearings. The spring-pad lubricator fit in a cellar at the bottom of each journal box. A felt pad with cotton wicks drew oil from the cellar, and this pad, held against the bottom of the axle bearing by a spring, lubricated the bearing. Supplementing the spring-pad lubricators on the driving journals was a Type DV-7 Nathan **mechanical lubricator**, operated by a connection to the reverse link, which distributed oil through tubes into a groove in back of the center of the crown bearing. Locomotives equipped with spring-pad lubricators were identified easily by a white star painted on the end of each driver axle, though in the waning years of steam, paint crews often omitted the star at shoppings. Spring-pad lubricators were removed from many tenders in the 1940s, and were replaced by conventional waste lubrication.

The **driving wheel** center castings were the standard spoked type used on the Espee. The wheel centers along with the steel tires were heat treated. The wheels had cast-on counterbalances with eight pockets in each

balance. These pockets were filled with lead as required to complete the counterbalancing after the wheels were mounted and tested for counterbalance and cross-counterbalance. Locomotives assigned to operate in mountain territory were equipped with small water lines to all wheels on the engine and tender. This **tire cooler system** kept the wheels from overheating under brake action on long descending grades by directing water over each wheel through a small nozzle. The engineer could open a valve to release the water spray if brakes were applied for extended times.

Another SP feature applied to the drivers and trailing truck wheels was their patented **tire safety clips**, which were welded on the inside and outside of the wheel center to prevent the tire from slipping off in the event of severe overheating due to prolonged braking.

Tire Clips per Sketch S-3653
2165

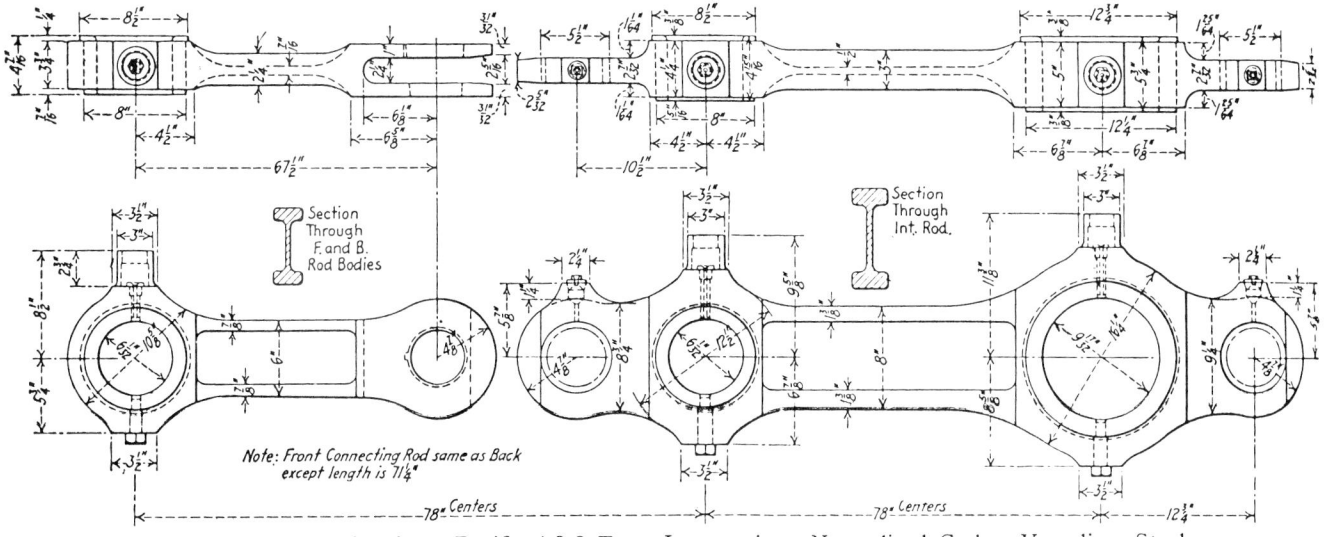

Side Rods for Southern Pacific 4-8-2 Type Locomotive. Normalized Carbon-Vanadium Steel.

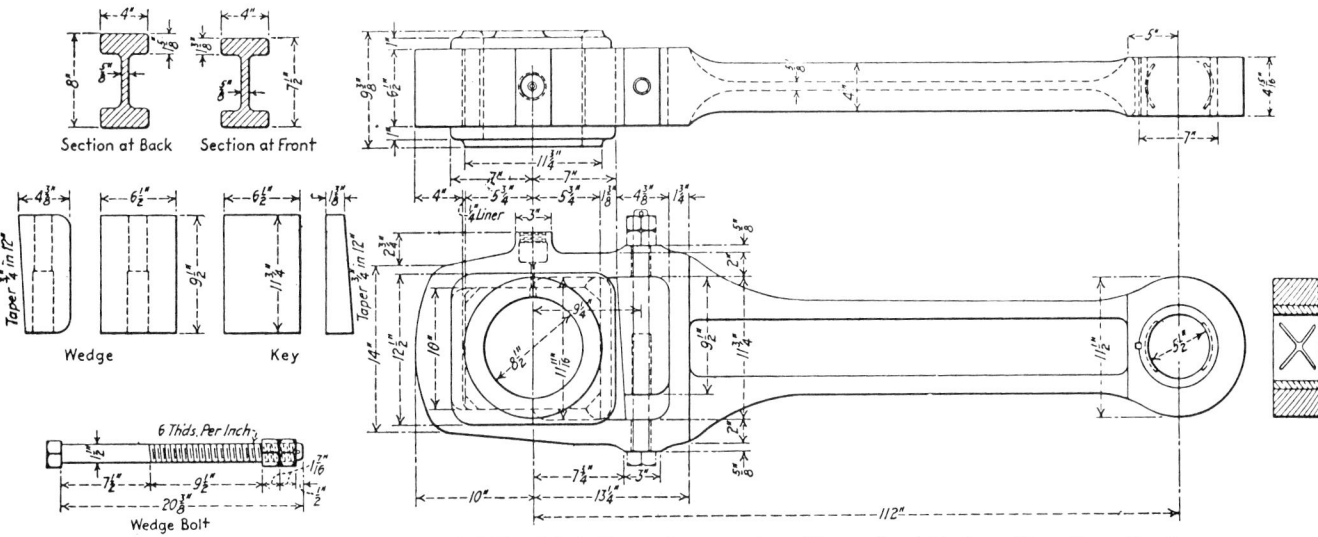

Main Rod for Southern Pacific 4-8-2 Type Locomotive. Normalized Carbon-Vanadium Steel.

In order to keep the dynamic augment to a minimum, the engines were equipped with **connecting rods** of normalized carbon-vanadium steel of I-section, hollow piston rods, and Z-type pistons, which provided for light reciprocating parts, 50 percent of which were balanced. The reduced section in the rods gave a total savings in weight of 1100 lbs. per locomotive, taking into consideration the amount of counterbalance weight also not needed. The total weight of reciprocating parts was 1,830 lbs., or one pound to each 201 lbs. of the total weight of the locomotive in working order, as compared with the ratio of 1 to 160, which was considered good practice at that time. The driving axles and main crankpins of heat-treated steel were hollow bored to achieve further, considerable weight reduction. The savings in weight of rods and counterbalances, combined with the corresponding decrease in rail pounding due to centrifugal counterbalance

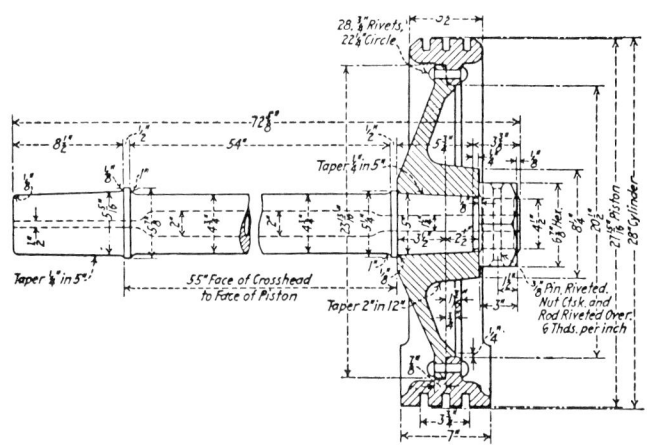

Hollow Piston Rod and Built-Up Z-Type Piston for Southern Pacific 4-8-2 Type Locomotives. American Locomotive Company.

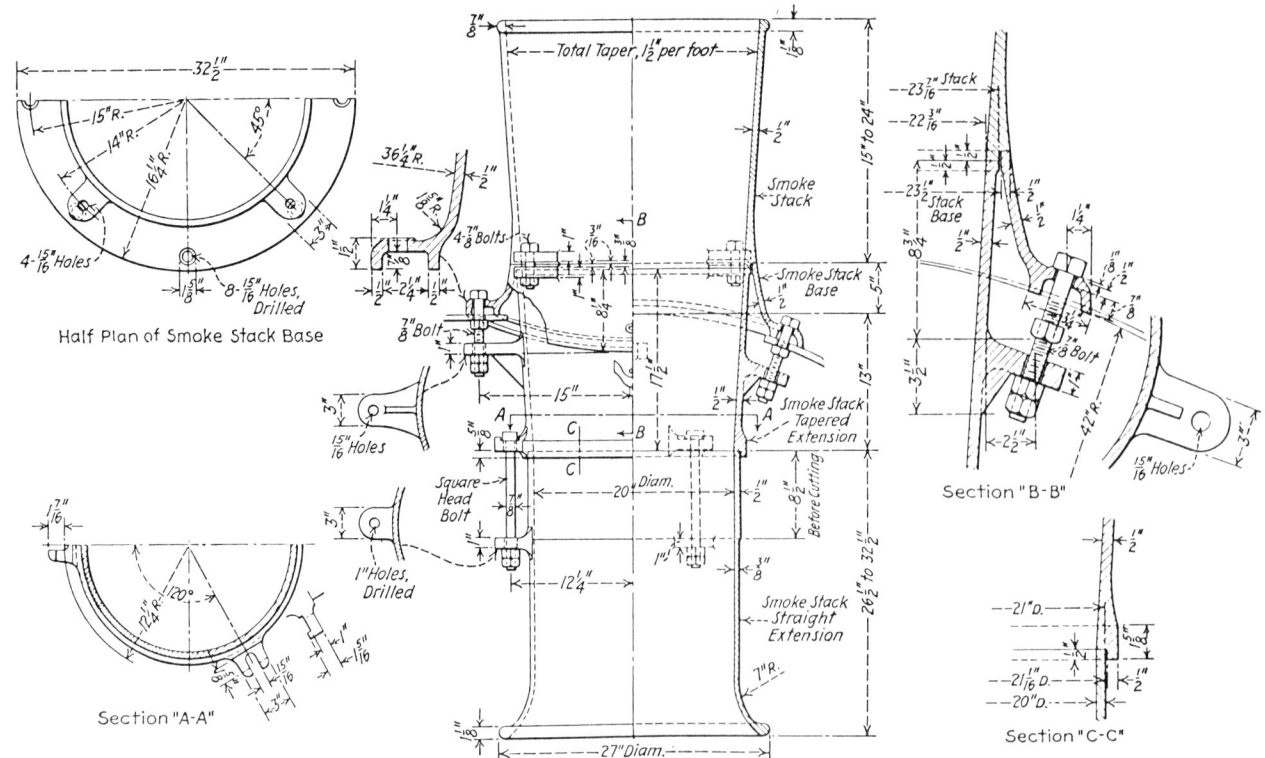

Total Taper, 1½" per foot
Smoke Stack
Smoke Stack Base
Smoke Stack Tapered Extension
Smoke Stack Straight Extension
Before Cutting
Square Head Bolt
1" Holes, Drilled
15/16" Holes
Half Plan of Smoke Stack Base
4-15/16" Holes
8-15/16" Holes, Drilled
Section "A-A"
Section "B-B"
Section "C-C"
Stack Base

Cast Iron Taper Smoke Stack with Inside Extension. Made in Four Pieces. Southern Pacific.

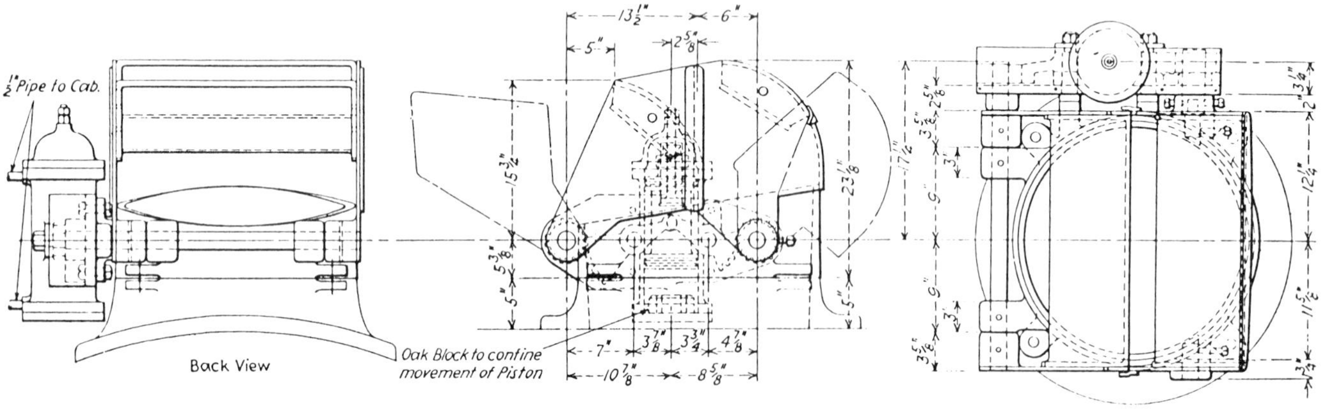

½" Pipe to Cab.
Back View
Oak Block to confine movement of Piston

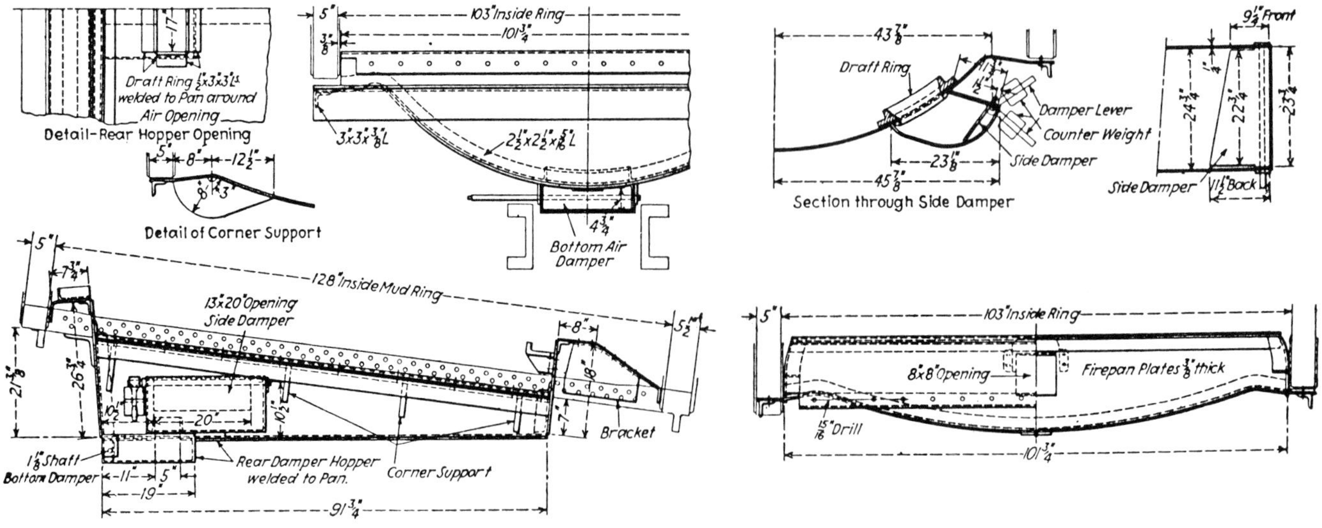

Draft Ring ½x3x3⅛L welded to Pan around Air Opening
Detail-Rear Hopper Opening
Detail of Corner Support
103" Inside Ring
Bottom Air Damper
Draft Ring
Damper Lever
Counter Weight
Side Damper
Section through Side Damper
9¼" Front
11½" Back
128" Inside Mud Ring
13"x20" Opening Side Damper
Bracket
1⅛" Shaft Bottom Damper
Rear Damper Hopper welded to Pan.
Corner Support
8"x8" Opening
Firepan Plates ⅜" thick
15/16" Drill

Standard Firepan. Southern Pacific

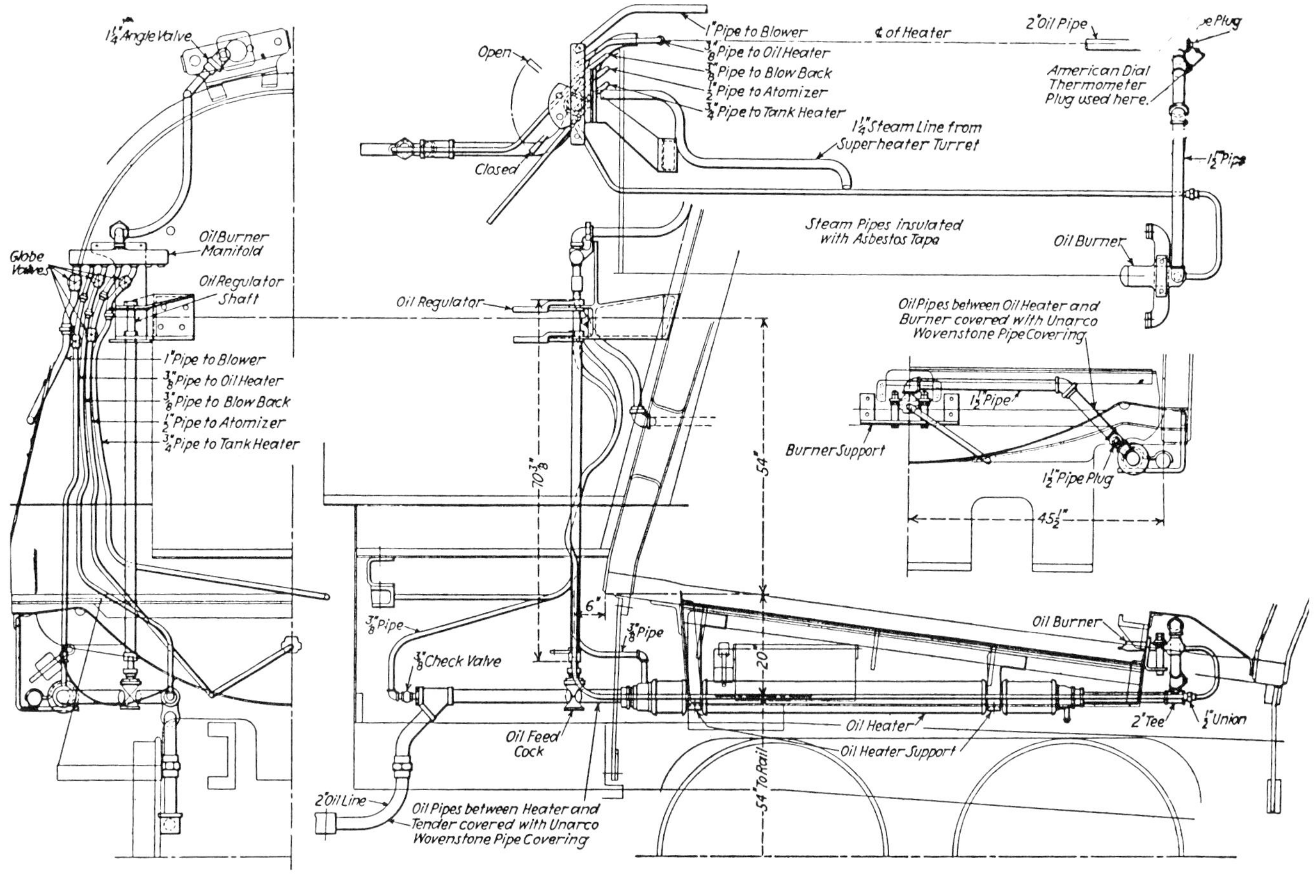

Standard Arrangement of Oil Burning Equipment and Piping. Southern Pacific.

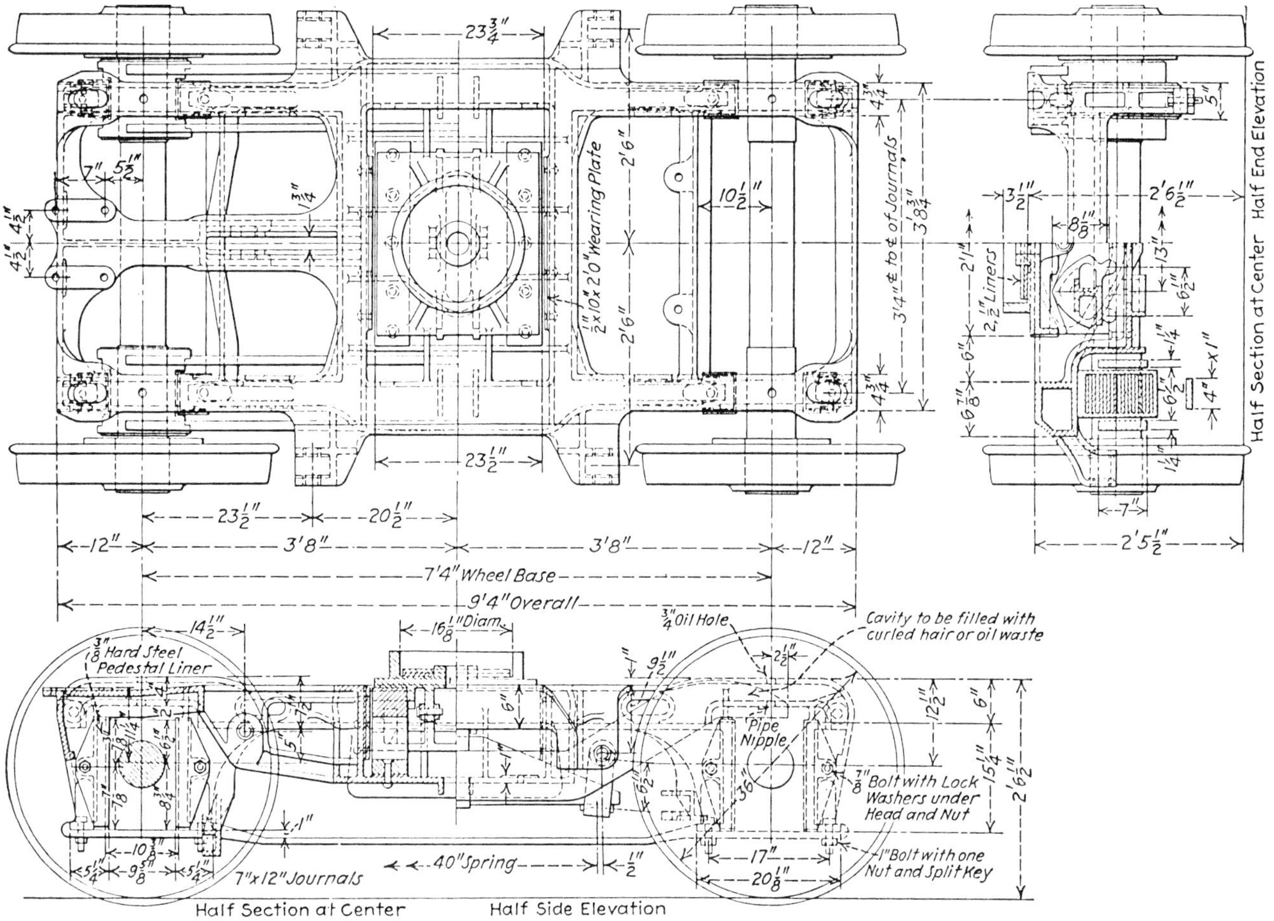

Economy Four-Wheel Leading Engine Truck with Constant-Resistance Renewable Centering Device
for Southern Pacific 4-6-2 and 4-8-2 Type Locomotives.   Commonwealth Steel Company.

Locomotive has been lifted off erecting floor blocks and will be moved by overhead crane to wheels. Note frame, rear buffer and housing for the two drawbars to tender, a safety feature. Note cab interior. That's an AC 2-8-8-2 receiving repairs in background.

Locomotive now in position over wheels. Excellent view of Delta trailing truck and booster engine. Note centering rocker device. A cast engine bed is in background for another 4-8-2 under construction.

The boiler is hoisted over the cast steel engine bed. The square bulge on the smokebox is for a superheater type that was used on some but not all of the Mt-4 class (see drawing on facing page). Note the staybolt pattern around the firebox and combustion chamber. Another Mt-4 is under construction in the background.

forces in wheels at high speeds, reduced the rail forces to about 450 to 650 lbs. per wheel.

The **spring rigging** was constructed to incorporate bent equalizers similar to those first used on 2-8-2 locomotives placed in service by SP twenty years earlier. This equalizer design provided a more stable construction by keeping the spring rigging in alignment, particularly on the 4-8-2 type. On lighter power this type of equalizer was not essential, and the advantage of its use was for some time practically overlooked. The common fault of earlier 4-8-2 designs was the drooping of the rear end of the engine. The Espee's installation of the bent equalizers overcame this trouble.

Westinghouse No. 6 ET **brake equipment** was applied, with air supplied by an 8½-inch cross-compound compressor on all classes except the Mt-2 and Mt-5, which had two cross-compound compressors. All engine wheels were equipped with single clasp brakes, while the tender trucks had two brakeshoes per wheel instead of one, located on each side of the wheel.

This made a more efficient brake and reduced wear to both shoes and wheels.

The Mt class locomotives were equipped with a two-wheel, Delta-type **trailing truck**. The term "delta" referred to the three-point loading on the truck. The frames were a one-piece steel casting incorporating pedestals, radius bar members and pin brackets, and rear centering device rocker pockets. These rear rockers provided a positive and smooth passage of the truck through curves, and stabilized the locomotive against nosing on curves and at high speed on tangent track.

The Franklin Railway Supply Company's **locomotive booster** was applied, the Mt-1 and 3's having type C-1 and the Mt-4 and 5's having type C-2. The booster engine was a separate two-cylinder steam engine geared to the trailing truck axle to assist the main engine in handling heavy trains, both in starting and on difficult grades. The steam supply was taken from the steam chest of the main cylinders instead of the steam dome. Superheated steam was thereby used instead of

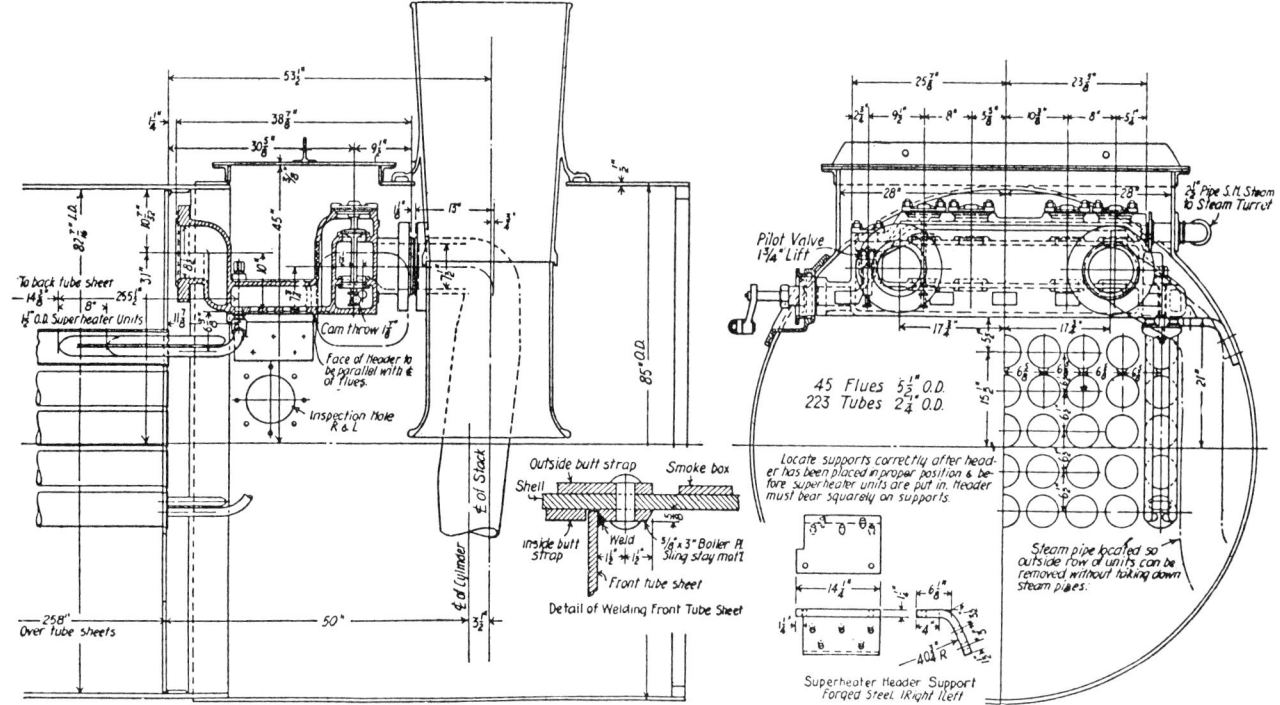

General Arrangement of Smokebox for Southern Pacific 4-8-2 (Mountain) Type Locomotive Equipped with Welded Flue Sheet and American Front-End Throttle Combined with Superheater Header. Built by Southern Pacific.

saturated steam, reducing steam consumption when operating the booster engine. The 1924-built 4-8-2's and 2-10-2's were the first SP engines on which superheated steam was used on the booster engine. The booster added an additional 10,160 lbs. of tractive effort to the locomotive. The booster was used only at low speeds where the engine was working hard with the reverse lever "in the corner" or the "company notch" for maximum power. When starting, the engineer would flip open the booster valve if he needed extra tractive effort. As the engine gained momentum, he would bring the reverse lever back towards center in working the cut-off. At a predetermined point on the quadrant the reverse lever would automatically shut off the booster valve at a speed of about 15 miles an hour. If the engine was working slowly on a heavy grade, the booster could be cut in below 15 miles per hour.

The **boiler** was designed with the largest proportions possible to obtain ample steaming capacity, and at the same time, to keep within safe limits of wheel load on the track. All the Mt's built for or by the Espee had a working boiler pressure of 210 lbs. per sq. inch. The boiler was conical, with an 84-inch outside diameter at the front barrel course, increasing to 95 inches at the combustion chamber course. The first course of the boiler shell was of $^{25}/_{32}$-inch steel and $^7/_8$-inch for the second and third courses, with the wrapper being $^1/_2$-inch thick. The boilers were equipped with two $3^1/_2$-inch pop **safety valves** of high relieving capacity.

The **firebox** measured $121^1/_{16}$ inches by 90 inches

inside of the sheets at the mud ring, and included a 75-inch long combustion chamber. The firebox and combustion chamber sheets were $^3/_8$ inches thick, except the inside throat connection which was $^9/_{16}$ inches thick, and were welded in construction. The firebox had an SP standard round-bottom firepan and was equipped with an oil heater and an SP-patented Von Boden-Ingles flat jet **oil burner**. As built, the primary air draft passed through a damper-controlled conduit at the burner. Secondary air was admitted below the firedoor. Modifications are discussed later.

The **boiler tubes** were 21 ft. 5 in. long and had installed within them a Schmidt-type **superheater** which consisted of 45 units, with a superheating surface of 1,162 sq. feet. The superheater increased the temperature of the steam to about 650°F, thus providing much more power from a given amount of steam.

A Worthington No. 4-B **feedwater heater** with a pump of 7,200 gallons per hour capacity was mounted on the left side of the boiler on Mt-1's. Class Mt-3 had the No. 4-BL type, along with Mt-4 engines 4346-4358. Locomotives 4359-4366 and the Mt-5's used the No. 4¼-BL. The BL unit was of the open type, where exhaust steam from the cylinders was condensed by, and actually mixed with the cold water from the tender, which was thereby heated to within a few degrees of the exhaust temperature. In closed-type heaters such as the Elesco and Coffin, heat exchanger tubes were used, but the tubes tended to choke with scale in bad water districts. SP had many bad water areas in desert divisions

View of Delta trailing truck and booster. Flexible pipe delivered steam to booster from the steam chest of the main cylinders. Cab markings indicate type, driver diameter, cylinder diameter over stroke, weight on drivers over booster truck weight, that engine had superheater and feedwater heater, and class of engine (see page 167). Note the starting valve for the Nathan non-lifting injector ahead of cab. Guy Dunscomb collection.

and surprisingly, even on some mountain divisions.

The Worthington heater had two pumps, one to boost cold water to the heater spray chamber, and one to move heated water through the check valve into the boiler. By using exhaust steam to preheat the water, savings of 12% fuel and 14% water were gained. The exhaust steam first passed through a check valve and an oil separator which, by means of a small drain, provided continuous and automatic elimination of lubricating oil before it entered the heating chamber.

A Nathan non-lifting **injector** was also provided for use under heavy working conditions or when the engine wasn't moving. On the Mt-1 the Worthington pump fed the check valve on the left side. The Nathan injector was on the right side, was operated by the engineer, and fed into a boiler check valve on the right side.

On Mt-3, 4 and 5 engines, the injector was mounted on and injected into the left side, so the fireman could operate it. The feedwater heater piping crossed under the boiler and fed the check valve on the right side.

The locomotives were fitted with a light design of Walschaert **valve gear**, positioned by an Alco type-E air-actuated **power reverse** with an emergency steam connection, which was lubricated by Alemite fittings.

The **sand box** was of large capacity and was mounted on the first boiler course. Two lines on each side fed sand when needed to the track ahead of the second and third set of drivers. The **steam dome** was on the second or conical course. On the Mt-1's the throttle controlled a valve in the dry pipe that came from the steam dome. Mt-4 and -5 engines had **front end throttles** which opened valves directly in the su-

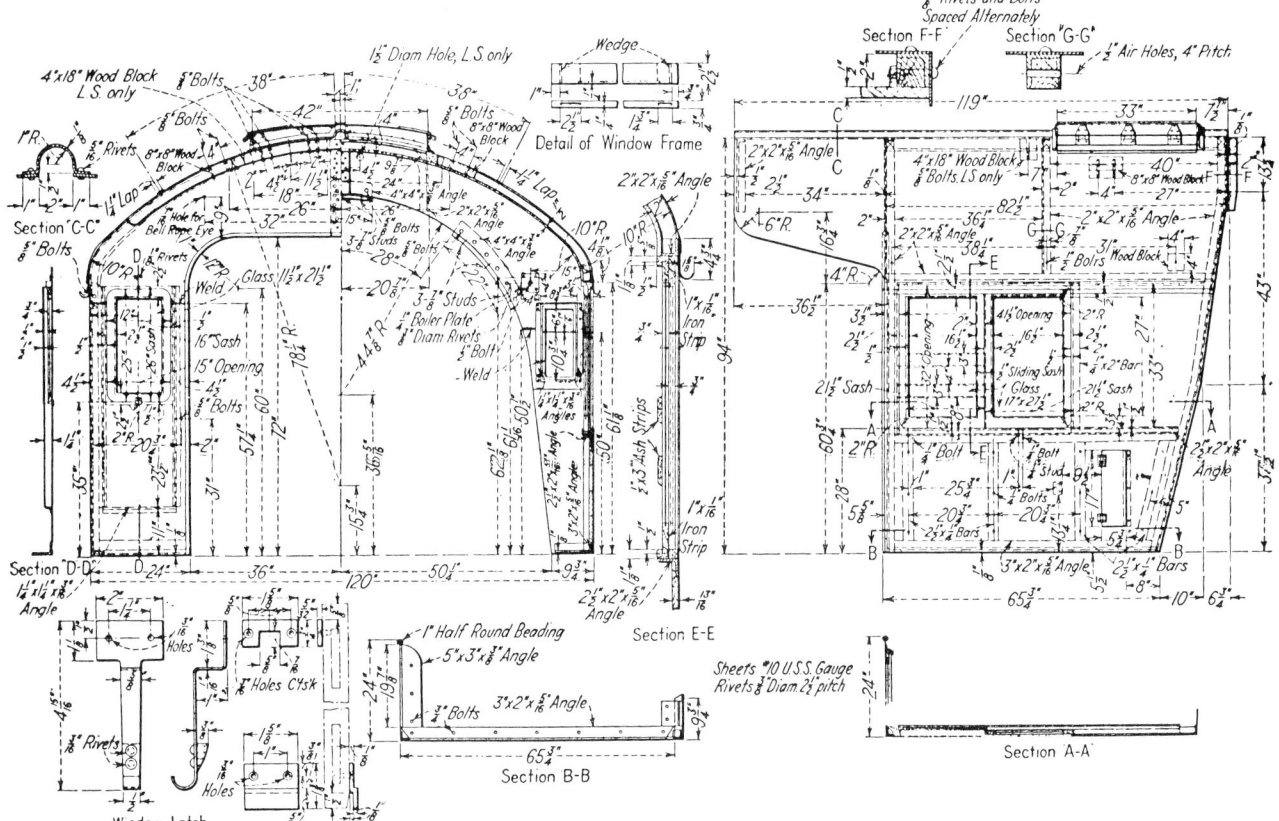

Cab for 4-8-2 Type Locomotive. Southern Pacific.

perheater header. The linkage was evident on the right side of the boiler.

The Nathan **whistle** had either 5 or 6 chimes (both types were used) and was controlled with a rod and lever linkage. The most common frequency of notes used on larger SP power with six chimes was the following notes, starting in the middle octave: C#, D#, F, G, A#, C#. Many larger engines, including the cab-forwards, had a five-chime whistle, again in the middle octave: C#, D#, F, A, D#. Both whistle types gave a very melodious and haunting tone, especially when the engineer varied the amount of steam with the lever rod.

The **headlight** applied to early SP-built Mt's apparently was a Sacramento shop design, with an 18-inch lens like the Sunbeam units applied to Mt-1's, but with a flared mounting base and side number boards.

The **cab** on the 4-8-2's was stated by SP to be shorter and slightly narrower than had been standard on earlier power, thus giving another source of weight reduction, about 200 lbs. By placing the steam turret on the outside of the cab at the front, it was possible to make some reduction in the cab length. By eliminating the two doors at the front, which with large-size boilers were too narrow to be practical, additional weight was saved. However, a window at the front on each side was retained. The steel cab floor was extended out as a run-

ning board along the cab side, and hand holds were located near the eaves to enable enginemen to pass around the outside of the cab to and from the boiler running boards. The front edge of the Mt-1 cabs was vertical, but on all other Mt locos it was sloped forward. This facilitated inspection and replacement of staybolts on the firebox without removal of the cab.

These 4-8-2 locomotives had a total weight of 368,000 lbs. of which 246,000 lbs. were on the drivers. The maximum tractive effort was 67,660 lbs. with the booster, and 57,510 lbs. without the booster, the factor of adhesion for the drivers being 4.28. Using Cole's ratio as a basis of comparison, they had a maximum horsepower capacity of 2,965 and a boiler capacity of 103.4 percent including the increase obtained by the use of the feedwater heater. This high percentage of boiler capacity indicated that the boiler could easily supply the cylinders at high speeds without forcing.

The new Mt class 4-8-2 that rolled out of the builder's erecting shops was indeed a product of the very latest steam locomotive construction, refinements and engineering. So well did the SP 4-8-2 design handle under greatly varying conditions of operation, that many enginemen considered the 4300s the best all-around working locomotive on the entire Southern Pacific roster. ∎

Cab interior — reverse quadrant and brake stand lower right foreground, throttle above. Boiler pressure and air brake pressure gauges in center. Oil firing valve, damper control valve, Blower, FW heater, atomizer, oil tank heater valves. Turret valves at top.

Locomotive 4344 slowly being lowered onto its wheels. The foreman uses a whistle to signal the overhead crane operator. The pilot truck pin was held upright as the engine inches down.

Main driver journals are aligned as the frame drops into position.

The new 4344 in service on the "Shasta" at Portland Union Station. Guy Dunscomb photo.

Three sections of the *Golden State Limited* are nearly ready to depart Los Angeles Central Station behind brand-new Mt-1 4-8-2's. SP photo.

Mt-1
4300 – 4327

BUILT 1923-24

GAUGE OF TRACK	DRIVING WHEEL DIAMETER	FUEL	CYLINDERS		BOILER		FIREBOX	
			DIAMETER	STROKE	DIAMETER	PRESSURE	LENGTH	WIDTH
4'-8½"	73"	OIL	28"	30"	84"	210 lbs.	121-1/16	90"

WHEEL BASE		TRACTIVE POWER			BOILER CAPACITY	TUBES		
DRIVING	ENGINE	MAIN CYLINDERS	BOOSTER	COMBINED		NUMBER	DIAMETER	LENGTH
20'-0"	42'-3"	57,510 lbs.	10,150 lbs.	67,660 lbs.	92.4%	223'-2¼"	45'-5½"	21'-6"

AVERAGE WEIGHT IN WORKING ORDER, LBS.				GRATE AREA SQ. FT.	HEATING SURFACES, SQUARE FEET				
ON DRIVERS	FRONT TRUCK	TRAILING TRUCK	ENGINE LOADED		TUBES	FIREBOX	EVAPORATING	SUPERHEATER	COMBINED
246,000	61,500	60,500	368,000	75	4,201	355	4,556	1,133	5,689

THE YEAR 1923 found the Southern Pacific taking delivery of 50 new locomotives. This huge order closely followed the 1922 delivery of the famed "Prosperity Special," when 20 of an order of 50 2-10-2 locomotives from Baldwin were sent west in a solid train. The "Prosperity Special" was run to boost national morale and trust in the economy, and attracted countrywide attention. The fact that these 50 2-10-2's had cost the SP $4 million showed the nation that the railroads were ready for big business.

Now, as part of SP's continuing effort to increase the total tractive power of its locomotive roster, the 1923 order contained 34 additional engines of the mammoth 2-10-2 type. Six heavy 4-6-2's were ordered, and 10 engines were to be the new 4-8-2 Mountain-type passenger locomotives. Also announced in the 1923 equipment program for Pacific Lines was $3.5 million for 141 new passenger cars and $7.8 million for 4,225 new freight cars, exclusive of refrigerator cars; and a half interest in $18 million for 5,330 new refrigerator cars ordered by Pacific Fruit Express, jointly owned by Southern Pacific and Union Pacific.

The Schenectady Works of American Locomotive Co. outshopped the first 10 Mt-1's and delivered them to Southern Pacific at El Paso, Texas, in December, 1923. The railroad deadheaded them west to the Los Angeles General Shops. After being set up there, the engines were first broken in and tested in freight service. They were then placed on local passenger runs for a short time so that the engine crews might become thoroughly familiar with them before attempting the record-setting, 815-mile run over the deserts and mountains between Los Angeles and El Paso. When officials felt the new engines were sufficiently broken in, five Mt's were sent to El Paso to await the through run to and from the Pacific Coast.

Appropriate ceremonies, attended by railroad and civic representatives, were held at Los Angeles on Jan. 6,

Train No. 25, the *Owl*, pauses at Berkeley before making the short run to Oakland, its final destination. August 24, 1940. Guy Dunscomb collection.

1924, when the newest "Leviathans on the rails" were dedicated to their important service. Engine 4302 had the honor of powering the first train east. The sparkling locomotive backed into Los Angeles Central Station and coupled onto train No. 4, the *Golden State Limited*. Set up alongside was 4-4-0 No. 1471. Now relegated to local service, the 1471 was, a comparatively few years earlier, the "pride of the rails," and was a striking comparison to the giant 4-8-2. Mrs. T.H. Williams, wife of the Assistant General Manager, broke a bottle of Cali-

fornia orange juice (Prohibition was four years old) over the right cylinder of 4302, and, whistle blowing, the train eased out of the station, starting a new era in SP locomotive operations.

The next 18 Mt-1 locomotives, Nos. 4310-4327, were delivered in May, 1924, and were also set up at Los Angeles. Placing them in service released a large number of older engines for lighter passenger service or freight duty, and added to SP's ability to keep pace with its constantly increasing traffic demands. ∎

In June, 1951, engine No. 4311 was in San Francisco commuter service. D.S. Richter photo.

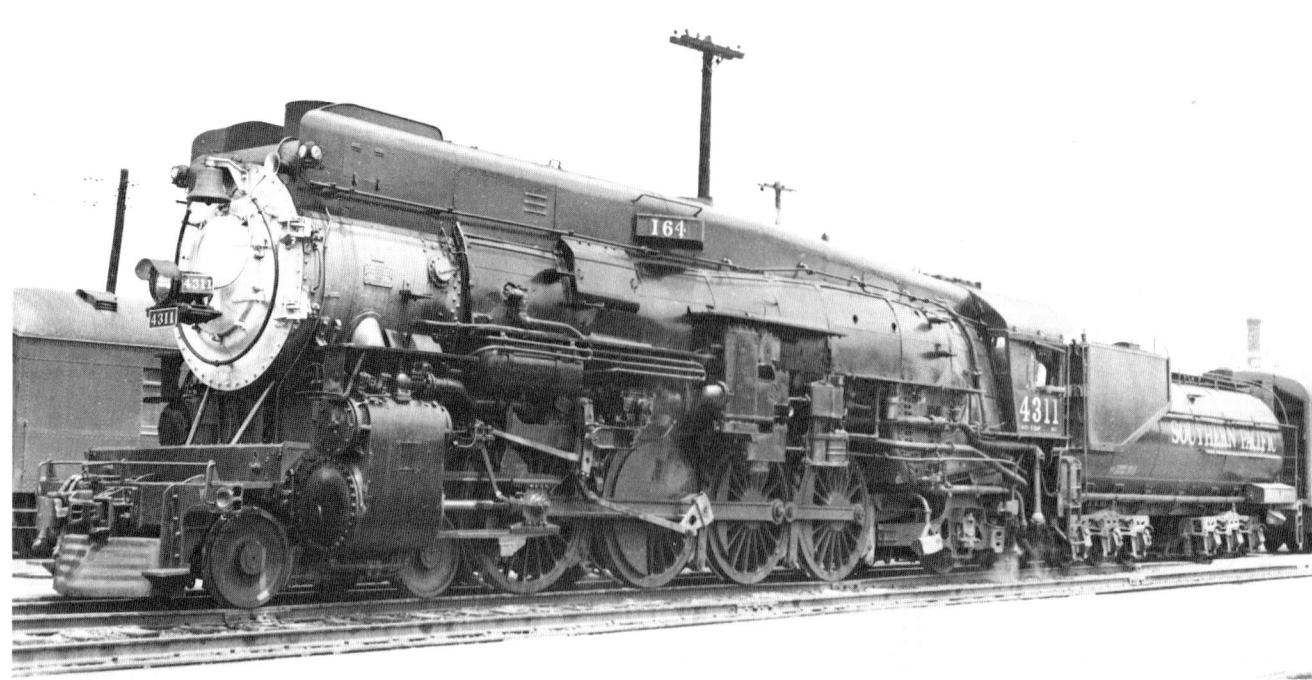

The first 10 Mt's, though delivered with Class 120-C-2 tenders having 4-wheel trucks, received 120-C-3 tenders with 6-wheel trucks during 1924. These were better suited to high-speed runs. Guy Dunscomb collection.

Above – Locomotives assigned to mountain divisions had snowplow pilots and a clamshell exhaust deflector. The deflector directed the exhaust back and kept it from blasting the roofs of snowsheds and tunnels. Here No. 4313 is on the *West Coast Limited* at Klamath Falls, Ore., May 30, 1939. H.B. Miller photo.
Below – 4318 is fitted for mountain service and has a 120-C-6 tender. Klamath Falls, July 6, 1939. F. Smith photo.

Above – No. 4323 has just received a skyline casing at this October, 1940, shopping. Mt's began receiving casings in February, 1939, the 4315 being the first so equipped. Guy Dunscomb collection.

Below – A unique engine because of its small smokebox door; no other known Mt photo shows such a door. How long No. 4321 kept it isn't known. Note Universal main driver replacement. West Oakland, Nov. 9, 1952. Frank Saarni photo, A. Menke collection.

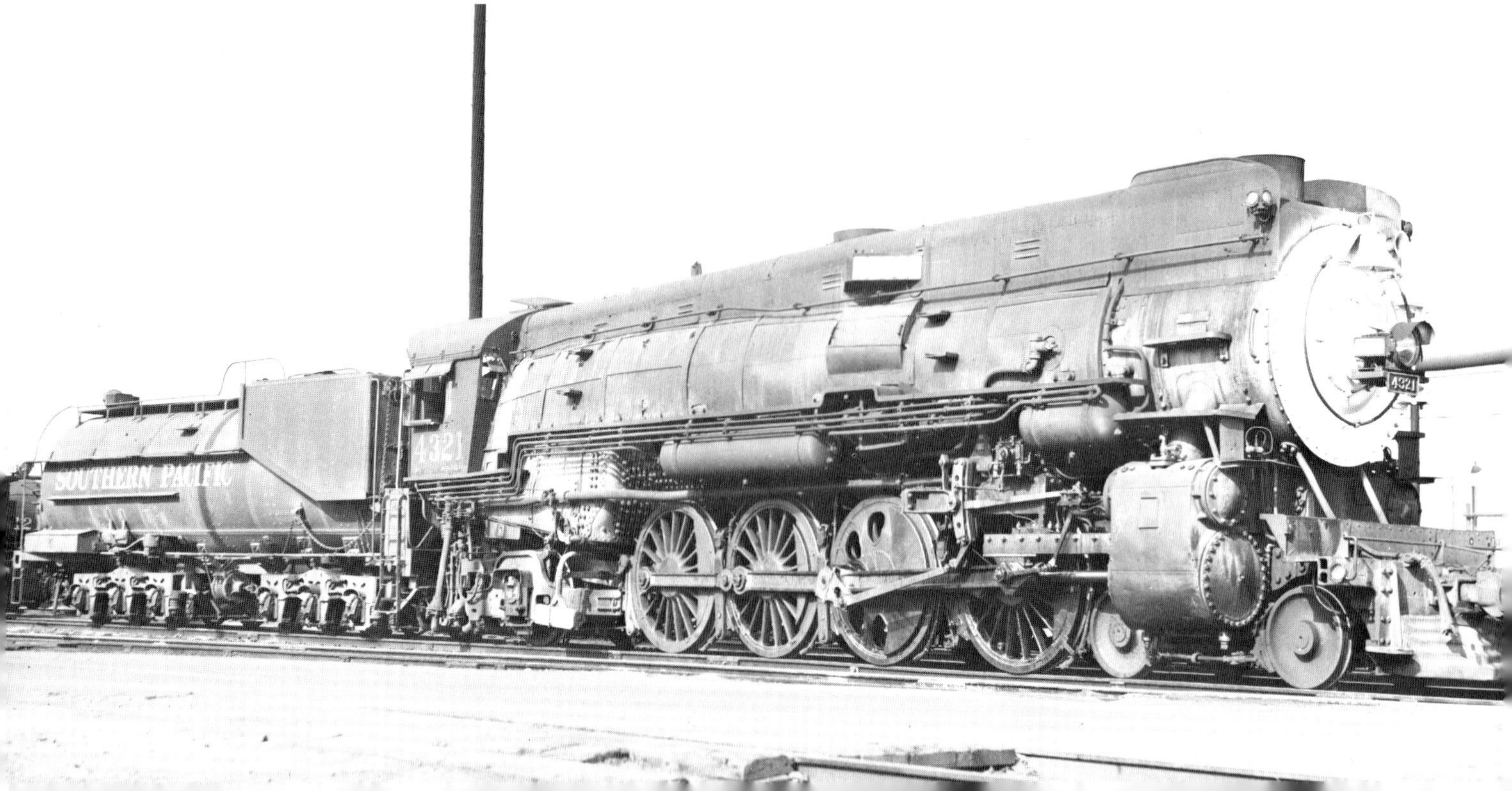

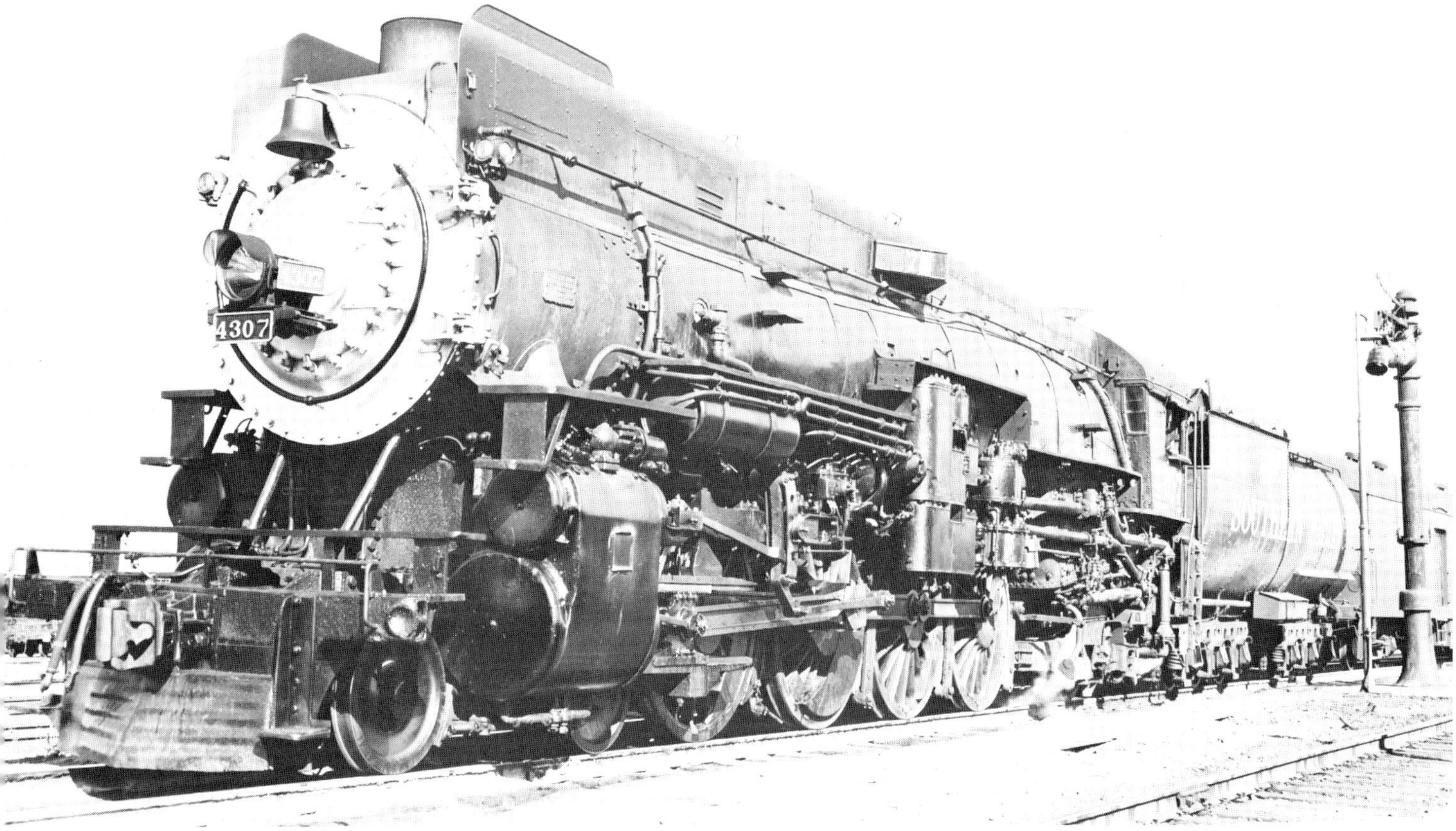

Above – Locomotive 4307 has the standard sheet-steel pilot which was first applied in the late 1940s. Watsonville Junction, Nov. 7, 1948. W.C. Whittaker photo.

Left – No. 4310 backing down to couple onto No. 201, a Gerber-Sacramento local. Main driver is a Universal replacement. Gerber, April 29, 1951. W.C. Whittaker photo.

Below – Freshly shopped No. 4320 at Fresno. Tender is Class 120-C-5. Nov. 30, 1939, H.B. Miller photo.

The head end brakeman checks the swaying high cars as Extra 4332 hammers through a reverse curve near Selby, Ca. in May, 1946. W. Whittaker photo.

Mt-3
4328 - 4345

BUILT 1925-26

GAUGE OF TRACK	DRIVING WHEEL DIAMETER	FUEL	CYLINDERS		BOILER		FIREBOX	
			DIAMETER	STROKE	DIAMETER	PRESSURE	LENGTH	WIDTH
4'-8½"	73"	OIL	28"	30"	84"	210 lbs.	121'-1/16"	90"

WHEEL BASE		TRACTIVE POWER			BOILER CAPACITY	TUBES		
DRIVING	ENGINE	MAIN CYLINDERS	BOOSTER	COMBINED		NUMBER	DIAMETER	LENGTH
20'-0"	42'-3"	57,510 lbs.	10,150 lbs.	67,660 lbs.	92.4	223'-2¼"	45'-5½"	21'-6"

AVERAGE WEIGHT IN WORKING ORDER, LBS.				GRATE AREA SQ. FT.	HEATING SURFACES, SQUARE FEET				
ON DRIVERS	FRONT TRUCK	TRAILING TRUCK	ENGINE LOADED		TUBES	FIREBOX	EVAPORATING	SUPERHEATER	COMBINED
246,000	'61,500	60,500	368,000	75	4,201	355	4,556	1,133	5,689

IN OCTOBER, 1872, the first new locomotive, Central Pacific 173, emerged from the General Shops at Sacramento for service on the present Southern Pacific Lines. The little 4-4-0, big in its time, was a beautiful machine, glistening with brass trim and jacket bands, an elaborate brass builder's plate between the mud

Central Pacific 173 as a coal-burner in 1881, minus much of its original trim. Photo at Sacramento by George Stoddard and Ira A. Todd.

guards, numbers and lettering in red shaded with green and gold, broad stripes of gold edged with green and red around the tank and domes, cab grained and varnished, and a beautiful painting of the Yosemite Valley on each side of the headlamp.

Building this locomotive inagurated a major Sacramento industry, ranked as the greatest locomotive shop in the West. During 53 years from 1872 to 1925, some 142 locomotives were built at Sacramento by a work force of 3100 craftsmen. Just since 1917, 63 engines had been built, including heavy 4-6-0 and modern 4-6-2 passenger locomotives, and also 0-6-0, 0-8-0 and 2-8-0 switching and freight engines.

Orders to outshop a massive block of 49 4-8-2's created the largest group of any one locomotive type SP ever attempted. The first of these, No. 4328, was completed Sept. 30, 1925. The locomotive was placed on display outside the shops for official company photos taken by D.L. Joslyn, an SP draftsman who photographed the cavalcade of new and rebuilt locomotives for 30 years before retiring in 1948. His legacy of beau-

No. 4328 exhibits the McCormick short pilot and a large "Sacramento" headlight.

tiful 8 x 10 negatives has contributed much to any SP motive power history. The locomotive was ceremoniously christened in the presence of SP officials, shop personnel, businessmen and civic leaders.

No. 4329 was completed Oct. 28,1925, and was followed by two engines per month until June,1926, when 4345 rolled out, completing 18 members of Class Mt-3 at a cost of $1.5 million. ∎

Above — Worthington feedwater heater and cross compound air pumps on left side. Nathan non-lifting injector ahead of cab. Large pipe from steam chest is to booster engine. The other large pipe is cold water to feedwater heater. Both photos, Guy Dunscomb collection.

Below — Alco power reverse gear was on right side. Nathan mechanical lubricator was mounted on valve gear support frame. Note at this time the blow down shot steam straight out to the side. Blow down spreaders were added in 1942.

Above – The first Mt-3. Note lady "engineer." The paint scheme is described on pages 78-79.

Left – Last Mt-3 on display at Salem, Ore., when new.

Below – No. 4336 on the *Oregonian*, fitted for assignment to mountain districts. Klamath Falls. April 10, 1938. H.B. Miller photo.

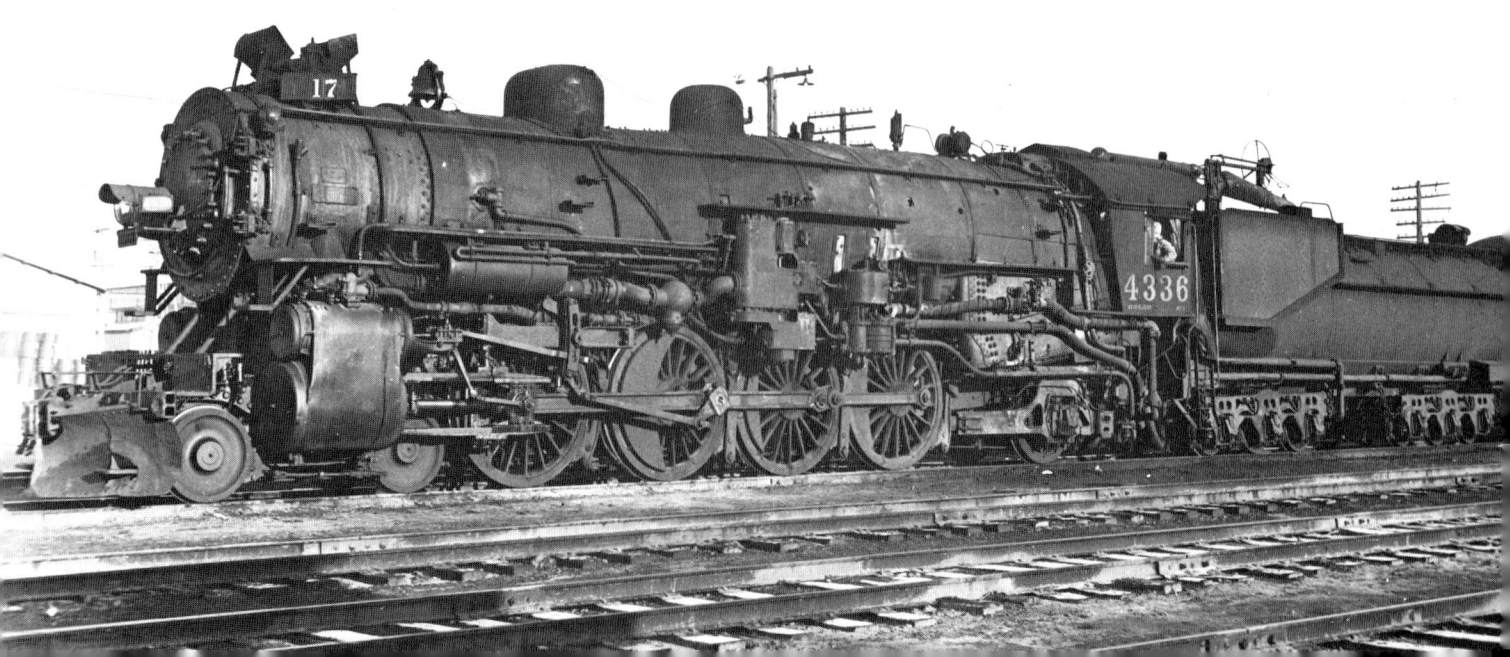

Above – Freshly shopped No. 4335 with new skyline casing applied. Photo shows original location of train indicator boards. They were moved back to mid-boiler in 1943, where it was easier for passing crews to read, being away from headlight glare. Sacramento, April 25, 1940. Guy Dunscomb collection.

Below – Classic pose of a capable engine. In this photo, No. 4334 stands at Dunsmuir. Smokebox front is standard silver, but sides of smokebox, as well as firebox, are graphite. Multiple-bearing crosshead guides, 160-C tender, and a Universal disc main driver have been appplied. The train in the background is likely the *West Coast*. Stan Kistler photo.

Note the location of the bell in this photo. The first engines outshopped with the skyline casing had the bell mounted here below the smokebox. It was soon decided to place it at the top of the smokebox for better audibility. Locomotives assigned to deluxe trains often received the white trim as seen here. Smokebox side and firebox in graphite. Smokebox front was silver. Sacramento, Guy Dunscomb collection.

Above — November, 1938, photo shows the 4328 with pilot and stack modifications and the larger 16,000 gallon tender. Oakland roundhouse. H. Miller photo.

Below — 4339 looks rather naked without exposed sandpipes and bell mounted low. Mojave, July, 1941. A Menke collection.

Extra 4366 shows what she's made of as she races heavy tonnage through Lathrop in the Central Valley. What a sight! February, 1951.   Guy Dunscomb photo.

Mt-4
4346 - 4366

BUILT 1926-29

GAUGE OF TRACK	DRIVING WHEEL DIAMETER	FUEL	CYLINDERS		BOILER		FIREBOX	
			DIAMETER	STROKE	DIAMETER	PRESSURE	LENGTH	WIDTH
4'-8½"	73"	OIL	28"	30"	84"	210 lbs.	121'-1 1/16"	90"

WHEEL BASE		TRACTIVE POWER			BOILER CAPACITY	TUBES		
DRIVING	ENGINE	MAIN CYLINDERS	BOOSTER	COMBINED		NUMBER	DIAMETER	LENGTH
20'-0"	42'-3"	57,510 lbs.	10,150 lbs.	67,660 lbs.	92.3%	223'-2¼"	45'-5½"	21'-5½"

AVERAGE WEIGHT IN WORKING ORDER, LBS.				GRATE AREA SQ. FT.	HEATING SURFACES, SQUARE FEET				
ON DRIVERS	FRONT TRUCK	TRAILING TRUCK	ENGINE LOADED		TUBES	FIREBOX	EVAPORATING	SUPERHEATER	COMBINED
246,000	61,500	60,500	368,000	75	4,191	355	4,546	1,133	5,679

ONLY TWO MONTHS separated the outshopping of the last Mt-3 and the first Mt-4, No. 4346, which officially entered the roster in September, 1926. The Mt-4's were identical to the Mt-1's and 3's in almost all specifications, though three modifications warranted a new class designation. A slightly larger Worthington feedwater heater, the 4¼-BL type, was used on engines 4359-4366. The first 13 engines of the class used a 4-BL type, as had the Mt-3. All Mt-4's were equipped with Franklin C-2 boosters; earlier 4-8-2's had C-1 boosters. The only major change that involved dimensions was the cab. The Mt-3's had a slanted front cab wall, designed to expose more firebox staybolts so that they could be replaced without removing the cab. On the Mt-4 and 5 classes the entire cab was moved back 12 inches, extending beyond the rear chafing iron. This allowed access to all staybolts along the firebox side.

Five of these engines, Nos. 4346-4350, were completed during September-November, 1926, and were first assigned to the Coast Division, making the entire 471-mile run from Los Angeles to San Francisco. They were used primarily on the *Lark,* or other first-class trains when not assigned to the *Lark.*

Engine 4350 received a little extra special treatment. The cylinder heads were chrome plated and the cab numerals and the "SOUTHERN PACIFIC LINES" lettering on the tender were applied as polished nickel-silver characters. The remaining 16 Mt-4's were completed in two blocks. Nos. 4351-4358 were put into service during September-December, 1927, and Nos. 4359-4366 between December, 1928, and March, 1929.

Also being built by Baldwin at this time were AC-4 class cab-forward simple articulated 4-8-8-2 locomotives. These engines, Nos. 4100-4109, were put into service in late 1928 and January, 1929. They had a new-style Vanderbilt tender with 16,000-gallon water capacity. The SP built tenders of this type at Los Angeles and Sacramento for the Mt-4's erected in 1928-29. ■

Outshopped in October, 1927, the 4353 clearly shows the color paint scheme used on many passenger locomotives at that time. It was also used on 4-6-0's and 4-6-2's. The smokebox and firebox were graphite. The boiler jacket, cylinder jacket, and wrapper around the air pump were grey-green. The cab roof reddish-brown. See the color photo in chapter 8. Guy Dunscomb collection.

Above – Newly-built 4364 has an exhaust splitter like those used on cab-forwards. It also has multicolor paint (see p. 78). 1929 photo.

Left – No. 4357 has been fitted with multiple-bearing crosshead guides. Sacramento, May 17, 1952. Both photos, Guy Dunscomb.

Below – No. 4363 rests beside the Roseville roundhouse in September, 1940. H.B. Miller photo.

On October 30, 1949, 4349 rests in front of the Gerber enginehouse, Note outside front-end throttle. Alan Aske photo.

These two views show changes that occurred over the years to engine 4346. The May, 1938 photo at Klamath Falls (above) shows it equipped for mountain district duty. The February, 1954 photo at Bakersfield (below) shows the skyline casing, multiple-bearing crosshead guide and Universal disc main driver. Both photos, H.B. Miller.

Above – The 51st Mt engine received extra touches when built. Boiler jacket and cylinder cover were gray-green (p. 78). The cylinder heads and the raised numerals and railroad name were polished nickel-silver. Superheater pipe atop boiler. Nov. 1926.

Below – Locomotive 4354 displays the wartime headlight and marker light shields in September, 1942. Note whistle position and exposed sand pipe valves. Both photos, D.L. Joslyn, Guy Dunscomb collection.

The 4348 received its rebuilding in December 1940. Train indicators were moved back to mid-boiler around 1943. Guy Dunscomb collection.

Between 1946 and 1951, five locomotives carried a *Daylight*-style paint scheme: Nos. 4350, 4352, 4353, 4361 and 4363. All were used on trains No. 51-52, the *San Joaquin Daylight*. Above – Bakersfield, Dec. 30, 1947. G.M. Best photo. Left – Modesto, 1947. Guy Dunscomb photo. Below – Los Angeles, 1947. Stan Kistler photo.

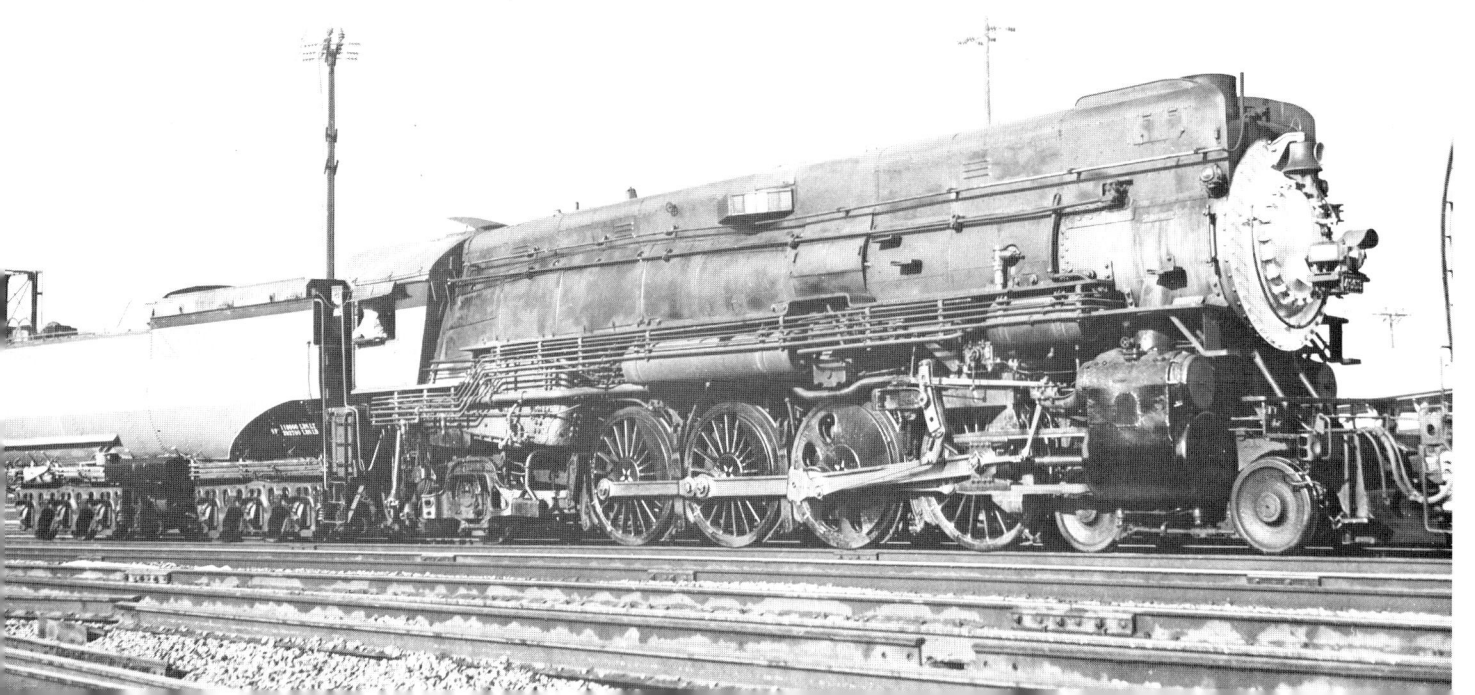

The first section of the westbound "Pacific Limited" works easily up the grade behind an Mt-5 in the Truckee River Canyon east of Boca. August 31, 1941. W. Whittaker.

Mt-5
4367 - 4376

BUILT 1929-30

GAUGE OF TRACK	DRIVING WHEEL DIAMETER	FUEL	CYLINDERS		BOILER		FIREBOX	
			DIAMETER	STROKE	DIAMETER	PRESSURE	LENGTH	WIDTH
4'-8½"	73"	OIL	28"	30"	84"	210 lbs.	121'-1/16"	90"

WHEEL BASE		TRACTIVE POWER			BOILER CAPACITY	TUBES		
DRIVING	ENGINE	MAIN CYLINDERS	BOOSTER	COMBINED		NUMBER	DIAMETER	LENGTH
20'-0"	42'-3"	57,510 lbs.	10,150 lbs.	67,660 lbs.	91.8%	220'-2¼"	45'-5½"	21'-6"

AVERAGE WEIGHT IN WORKING ORDER, LBS.				GRATE AREA SQ. FT.	HEATING SURFACES, SQUARE FEET				
ON DRIVERS	FRONT TRUCK	ENGINE LOADED	TRAILING TRUCK		TUBES	FIREBOX	EVAPORATING	SUPERHEATER	COMBINED
246,000	61,500	60,500	368,000	75	4,161	355	4,516	1,133	5,649

Demands on the motive power in the passenger train pool were still increasing systemwide in 1929. New name trains such as the *Gold Coast*, the *San Joaquin Flyer*, the *Cascade*, the *Klamath*, the *West Coast*, the *Apache* and the *Argonaut* were all added to an already impressive lineup of daily flagships that traversed the Southern Pacific's vast rail lines. The railroads at this time also carried nearly all transcontinental express and mail, so the ever-increasing demand for powerful, fast engines was not only to haul first-class passenger trains, but also mail and express trains.

The San Francisco General Offices placed an order with Sacramento Shops for ten additional Mt's. Because trains were getting longer and heavier, it was deemed practical to add an additional cross-compound air compressor to ensure adequate air build-up during prolonged braking. To balance the weight, the Worthington No. 4¼-BL feedwater heater was retained on the left side, but the two air pumps were mounted on the right side below the running board. The bell's location was changed on this class, now being mounted

on a bracket on the smokebox front. Other than these superficial changes, the engines, designated Mt-5, were identical to the Mt-4's. All had the 16,000-gallon cylindrical Vanderbilt tender when outshopped new.

Locomotive 4376 was officially placed on the roster March 30, 1930, and had the distinction of being the last completely new locomotive built by the Southern Pacific. On her smokebox she carried the SP Company builder's plate. These plates did not show the shop number (No. 4376 was designated No. 187) but only the date the locomotive was outshopped. The railroad became very involved in modernizing older freight locomotives, and all shop resources from then until the late 1930s were devoted to rebuilding and rejuvenating the old Mallet 4-6-6-2's and 2-8-8-2's to simple articulateds, and the building of eight heavy 0-8-0 switchers, using boilers from old A-3 "Atlantics." All but one of these switchers, numbered 1307-1314, were completed by March, 1931.

By 1931, the Depression was in full swing, and the plans to complete No. 1314 were laid aside. Six years

This 1943 photo shows the 4369 at Roseville with wartime headlight and classification light visors applied. Mt-5's were delivered with Pyle National headlights and with swing-type bells mounted at the smokebox top. On air-ringer bells applied to earlier locomotives, only the clapper moved. Note blowdown spreader has been applied. Al Phelps photo.

later, the last 0-8-0 locomotive was finally built, using A-3 No. 3067's boiler, and entered the roster in April, 1937. Though, strictly speaking, it was not a completely new locomotive, since a 4-4-2 boiler was used, the 1314 was a different wheel arrangement, and was officially the last of a long line of SP-built engines. Between 1872 and 1937, the company had turned out 248 engines for itself, and also built two 4-4-0's for the Virginia & Truckee. Of these locomotives, 197 were built at Sacramento. Two were built at Ogden in 1919, 14 at Los Angeles during 1917-28, 24 in Houston during 1921-30, and 11 at Algiers between 1919-21. Truly, though, the sleek, lanky 4-8-2's represented the zenith of the craftsmanship at the SP Shops in Sacramento, and also the best of the technical knowledge in the Mechanical Department at 65 Market Street, San Francisco. ■

It is July 12, 1937 in Ogden, and we see a resplendent 4376 simmering after having just delivered the inaugural eastbound *Forty-Niner* to the Union Pacific. The engine was assigned to the Salt Lake Division portion of that train's run for some time. Photographer unknown, A. Menke collection.

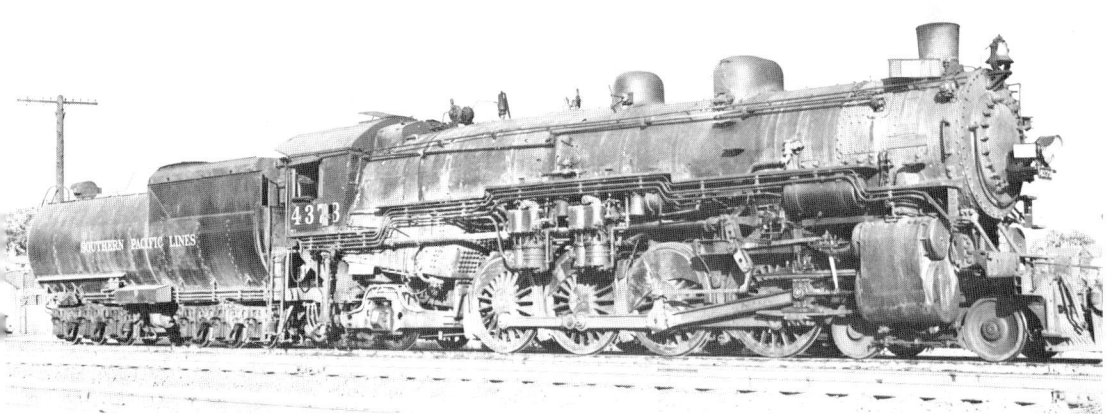

Top — In May, 1948, the 4371 awaiting to haul Oakland-Ogden local, had not yet received the skyline casing, has been modified little. Sparks.
Middle — The "Advanced Overland Limited" prepares to leave Sparks, May 29, 1937.
Bottom — 4373 awaits helper duty at Santa Margarita, July, 1941. Three photos, Guy Dunscomb collection.

Above — Right side had the two air pumps. Note Alco reverse year, throttle linkage, control rod for whistle. Note style of holes on trailing truck. There were five different patterns. See data, Chapter 11. Below — Superheated steam line running along top of boiler to turret. Note spoked trailing wheel.

Above – No. 4371 on the third section of symbol freight 423. Engine has clamshell exhaust deflector and 120-C-2 tender. Atwater, Oct. 3, 1953. A. Menke collection.

Below – No. 4369 in commute service, with multiple-bearing guides, Universal disc main driver, and 120-C-5 tender. San Francisco, May 16, 1952. R. Gray photo.

53

Two views of No. 4370. Above – The engine at Ogden in June, 1949, looks much as when it was built. Note the auxiliary water car, used when engines were in freight service on limited-water districts. Ice deck is in background. H.B. Miller photo.

Right – The engine ended service with this appearance, shown on the Gerber-Sacramento local. Note Universal disc main driver, multiple-bearing guides, and visor-less headlight. Gerber, June, 1951. W.C. Whittaker photo.

Left – The 4372 was at Fresno in March, 1948, and multiple-bearing guides and a 120-C-6 tender had been applied, but the engine would not receive a skyline casing until August, 1949.

Below – Freshly shopped No. 4374 waits to take out a westbound freight at Roseville in this 1945 view. Smokebox front is silver although this did not become standard until 1946. Al Phelps photo.

Mt-2 4386 works up the Sierra grade near Colfax as point helper on the eastbound "Overland" in this 1949 photo.

Mt-2
4385 - 4390

BUILT 1924

GAUGE OF TRACK	DRIVING WHEEL DIAMETER	FUEL	CYLINDERS		BOILER		FIREBOX	
			DIAMETER	STROKE	DIAMETER	PRESSURE	LENGTH	WIDTH
4'-8½"	73"	COAL	29"	30"	86'-⅛"	210 lbs.	126'-⅛"	96'-¼"

WHEEL BASE		TRACTIVE POWER			BOILER CAPACITY	TUBES		
DRIVING	ENGINE	MAIN CYLINDERS	BOOSTER	COMBINED		NUMBER	DIAMETER	LENGTH
19'-6"	43'-7"	61,273	NONE	NONE	88.9%	234'-2¼"	50'-5½"	22'-0"

AVERAGE WEIGHT IN WORKING ORDER, LBS.				GRATE AREA SQ. FT.	HEATING SURFACES, SQUARE FEET				
ON DRIVERS	FRONT TRUCK	TRAILING TRUCK	ENGINE LOADED		TUBES	FIREBOX	EVAPORATING	SUPERHEATER	ARCH TUBES SYPHONS —COMBINED—
262,500	65,500	63,000	391,000	84.7	4,599	345	4,942	1,380	6,440

THE EL PASO & SOUTHWESTERN had trackage from El Paso, southwest to Douglas, Arizona, and thence northwest to Tucson, a distance of 343 miles. From El Paso going east the line headed northeast to Santa Rosa, N. M. Trackage rights were leased from the Chicago, Rock Island and Pacific Railway between Santa Rosa and Tucumcari, N.M., a distance of 330 miles. The EP&SW then had its own trackage from Tucumcari north 132 miles to Dawson.

On Nov. 11, 1924, Southern Pacific took over control of the road and its lease agreement with the Rock Island. The newest of 143 steam engines which came with the property were six 4-8-2's, EP&SW Nos. 410-415, under construction at Alco's Brooks Works in Dunkirk, N.Y. The records show that the first two, outshopped by Brooks in September, 1924, were shipped on Oct. 3, 1924. They were set up during October by the EP&SW and were the only engines that could have actually operated under the EP&SW. The other four engines entered service in November, the same month SP acquired the road.

These engines were quite different from the SP Mt's in appearance, and in design and appliances applied. They were the heaviest Espee 4-8-2's, weighing 391,000 lbs., a good 23,000 lbs. heavier than other Mt's. The tractive effort, 61,273 lbs., was nearly that of Espee's GS-1 4-8-4's, rated at 62,200 lbs. without booster.

The **boiler** was conical, with an outside diameter of 84½ inches at the front barrel course, increasing at the combustion chamber to 94³/₁₆ inches. It was equipped with two high relieving capacity pop safety valves. The original boiler pressure was 210 lbs. per sq. in. The **firebox** was 126⅛ inches long by 96¼ inches wide inside the mud ring. A combustion chamber extended 65¼ inches into the boiler. The boiler tubes and **flues** were 22 ft. long. A Schmidt type-A **superheater** with 1380 sq. ft. of superheating surface was installed.

The firebox was also equipped with two Nicholson **thermic syphons** and three arch tubes. These funnel-shaped syphons drew cooler water from the front bottom area of the firebox to the top of the crown sheet. Their function was to circulate the water more effi-

A rare photo. On May 22, 1927, the SP ran an employee picnic special from El Paso to Alamagordo. A newspaper article reported "The train will be pulled by engine 4390, recently plated with brass." El Paso Shop Electrician R.A. Bowhay recalled that "it was trimmed and beautifully painted in brass from knuckle to knuckle with some chrome and black paint." Note small SP herald at the top of the smokebox, the solid trailing truck wheel, and that the standard SP platform steps replaced the ladders. The ladders were later re-applied, and spoked trailing wheels were also applied later. It appears that the piston covers and cylinder saddle were painted brass color, as well as the smokebox and boiler jacket. There is brass trim on the running boards and main reservoir straps. The main cylinder covers appear to be chrome or nickel. It must have been striking! Unfortunately, it did not last long. Guy Dunscomb collection.

ciently and to relieve stress by making temperatures more uniform. The syphons substantially braced the crown sheet, and they and the arch tubes supported the brick arch. The thermic syphons provided 94 sq. ft. of evaporating surface and the arch tubes added another 22 sq. ft. The firebox was designed to burn coal and the grates were fitted with a Franklin steam **grate shaker**. This device consisted of two operating air cylinders and a double control valve so any one section of the grates or combination of sections could be shaken at one time. The ashes dropped into a self-cleaning ashpan that was fitted with hoppers ahead and behind the trailing truck. Periodic elimination of ash gave better combustion and allowed longer locomotive runs.

Coal was delivered from the tender to the firebox by a "Type B" duPont-Simplex **stoker** made by the Standard Stoker Co. A single horizontal screw was driven by a small, two-cylinder steam engine. Distribution of coal in the firebox was accomplished by steam jets. The volume of coal fired was proportional to the speed of the screw, which was controlled by a stoker engine throttle operated by the fireman. The stoker engine was located below the cab deck on the left side.

The Elesco **feedwater heater** was used on these six locomotives. The SP had experimented with this type feedwater heater on two 2-8-2's and two 4-6-2's, but it was never adopted as practical because the railroad felt the Elesco type tended to clog too severely with hard water deposits. They were, however, retained for the life of the Mt-2's. Unlike the Worthington BL type, the Elesco heater was a closed system where the water to be preheated did not come in direct contact with the steam. Instead, the water passed through copper tubes, each tube traversing the heater unit four times before

Left – Original appearance shows boiler tube pilot, classification lights on smokebox front. Note Pyle headlight didn't have flared number plates.
Right – Rebuilt appearance. Note bell, classification light placement, different headlight with flared number plates, solid pilot, and incline of steps decreased. May 31, 1945. Guy Dunscomb photo.

going through the delivery pipe to the boiler check. The cold water pump for the feedwater heater was hung on the right side under the running board. Originally it was ahead of the first driver. The feedwater boiler check valve and injector boiler check valve were originally located at the top of the boiler ahead of the sand box.

The **cylinders** were fitted with Okadee pneumatic cylinder cocks. Valve motion was controlled by Baker **valve gear** and Alco pneumatic **reverse gear**. Piston speed was 1372 ft. per minute when the engine was running at 60 mph. Mt-2's had multiple-bearing **crosshead guides**. The multiple bearing surfaces in this type guide reduced wear compared to the alligator guide.

The rectangular **tenders** were built to carry 12,300 gallons of water and 20 tons of coal. They were also equipped with a rear vestibule which was intended to help stabilize the first car of a passenger train, but in practice, they had little effect. While the engines remained as coal burners, SP did little to modify them, but in the thirties, the engines underwent major changes to bring them into line with SP's own practice of steam design.

All the locomotives were first converted to oil, at the El Paso and Los Angeles Shops during 1929-30. The tender vestibules were removed at this time (some may have been removed earlier). The thermic syphons and arch tubes were removed from the firebox and a standard firepan and oil burner installed. Oil tanks were placed in the coal bunkers. The square shape of the oil tanks probably decreased the water capacity somewhat. The tender behind No. 4388 was wrecked and scrapped in 1934, and this engine received a 12,000-gallon Vanderbilt tank, the only engine of the class to be so equipped. During this same shopping, the two boiler check valves were moved from the top to one on each side of the boiler. Around 1937, the Espee installed **lateral driving boxes** on the front drivers. Note there was no space between the 1st and 2nd drivers, as on the other Mt's that came equipped with these devices.

In 1939-40 and 1942 the cylinders of these engines were bushed down to 28 inches diameter, and the boiler pressure was increased to 225 lbs. per sq. in. This increased tractive effort to 61,620 lbs. Between November, 1943 and June, 1944, El Paso Shops installed Walschaert valve gear to replace the Baker gear on all engines. The Elesco cold-water pumps were moved

Left side of 4386 clearly shows Baker valve gear and check valves on top of boiler ahead of sand box. Note steep incline of ladders. They were this way to allow enginemen access to train indicators. In the mid-1940s, indicators were moved behind the stack, and the incline decreased for safety. El Paso, September, 1937. Doug Richter photo.

back over the right rear driver and a second air reservoir was hung where the pump originally was.

Between 1942 and early 1943, El Paso Shops rebuilt the tenders again, this time increasing the water capacity to about 15,500 gallons. During these shoppings four of the engines received skyline casings, 4388 being the first; 4390 was the last of the six to receive a casing, in 1950. El Paso Shops also applied Universal disc main

drivers to some engines in 1947-48. The entire class was transferred to the Sacramento Division in 1948.

The engines worked in both freight and passenger service on the Sacramento Division. They became common as point helpers out of Roseville on passenger trains and express reefer trains east over "The Hill." On occasion they even roamed as far north as Portland, Oregon. All were off the roster by March, 1953. ■

Right side view of No. 4385. Note original cold water pump position ahead of first driver, and "chicken coop" cab roof hatch; these were removed in the late 1930s. Tender is original 123-R-1 configuration but converted to oil. Los Angeles, May, 1935. G.M. Best photo, A. Menke collection.

Mt-2's from the Sacramento Division sometimes strayed north to Oregon, as with 4389 at Portland on Sept. 10, 1949. D.H. Roberts photo.

No. 4388 was the only engine that used a 12,000-gallon cylindrical tank, its original tender having been wrecked and scrapped in 1934. Jim Bowie photo at El Paso, 1940. Guy Dunscomb collection.

No. 4388 in March, 1950, fresh out of the shops at Roseville. It was the first Mt-2 to receive a skyline casing, which occurred in 1941. Al Phelps photo.

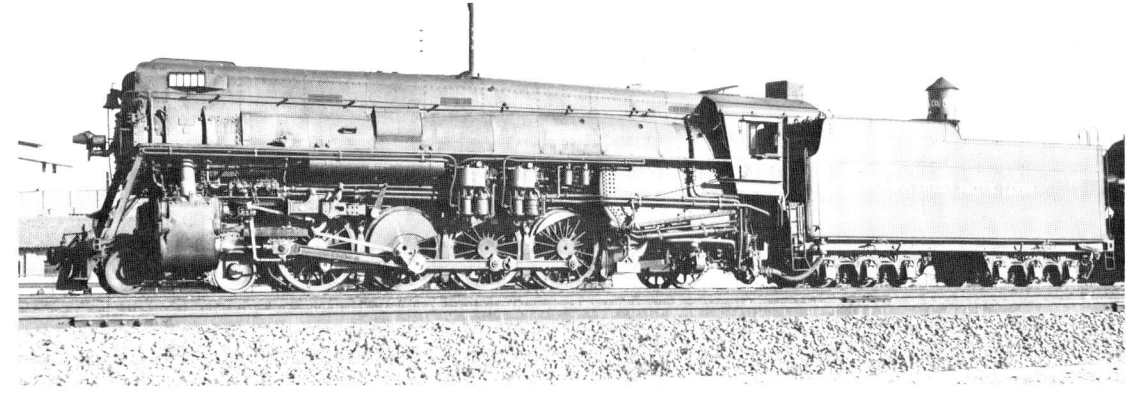

Tender No. 8581 on engine 4387 was the first to be enlarged to Class 160-R-1, at El Paso Shops in March, 1942. Photo taken April, 1942 at Los Angeles by G.M. Best.

A beautiful portrait of the 4390 at Norden, the summit of the Sierra's. It has helped the eastbound Overland and has been turned on the snowshed covered turntable. The four unit diesel has helped an eastbound freight. The steamer will couple to the units and lead them

Compare these two photos for changes that occurred over the years. The 4390, above, is largely as-built in this September, 1937 view at El Paso. Spoked trailing truck wheels and an oil bunker have been applied, and raised lettering (see p. 58) retained. Doug Richter photo.

No. 4389, below, has had the cold water pump moved back, a second air reservoir and Walschaert gear added, and with train indicators moved back, ladders are less steep. This was safer and gave better access to feedwater heater piping. Lordsburg, December, 1946. Al Phelps photo.

Maintenance
and Modifications

The 4318 has received skyline casing and new tender Sept. 30, 1940.

THE STEAM LOCOMOTIVE, a majestic machine born of man's ingenuity, was a creation that required meticulous and constant attention from its creators. The stresses of extreme variations in temperature, high pressures, and thousands of pounds of rotating and reciprocating parts all were inherent properties of the machine and tended to cause its own destruction.

Maintenance technology developed alongside the modern steam locomotive. Time lost in shopping was costly to the railroad and every means available was utilized to standardize time schedules for each class of repairs, shopping sequences, procedures, materials, and parts availability. In 1924, the company devised a scheduling system to be used by all major shops. Each class of repair had a set number of days for completion. Coordination between departments guaranteed that all

parts were ready and repair jobs completed on time. The incoming locomotives were set up on the schedule when due for repairs, and the operating department knew exactly when they would be returned to the motive power pool, as the date of repair completion could be predetermined.

Under the 1924 schedule system the Sacramento General Shops was able to increase the number of Class 2 repairs in 1923 from 78 at an average of 54 working days, to 92 at 41 working days. Class 3 repairs dropped from an average of 31 days to 26 days, and Class 4 and 5 repairs were cut down from 25 to 18 days. By 1940, many smaller, older engines had been retired and improved standardization and techniques reduced the working days per engine to 26 for Class 2 repairs, 21 days for Class 3, and 20 days for Class 4 repairs.

Tripped toes necessitate a shopping. Roseville, 1949, Al Phelps

SOUTHERN PACIFIC CLASSIFICATION OF STEAM LOCOMOTIVE REPAIRS

Class 5: Renewal of drivers, engine and trailing trucks, renewal and turning of tires, necessary repairs to machinery and tender.

Class 4: Same as Class 5, except also partial set of flues.

Class 3: Same as Class 5, with full set of flues.

Class 2: New firebox, or one or more shell courses, or roof sheet, flues new or reset, tires turned or new, general repairs to machinery and tender.

Class 1: Complete rebuild, new boiler or new back end, flues new or reset, tires turned or new, general repairs to machinery and tender.

The **boiler**, because it was subjected to such great variations of temperature and pressure, and thus expansion and contraction, as well as corrosive factors, required constant attention and maintenance. From the time the locomotive left the engine house these forces worked upon the boiler as it produced steam for the many and frequent operating variations due to grade, speed changes, and stops. When the throttle was opened, there was an immediate, powerful surge in the steam action of the water, especially over the firebox, where the temperature was highest. Water had to be injected into the boiler when running, the amount dependent on how hard the engine was working. This water, even that preheated in the feedwater heater, was 100 to 200°F cooler than water in the boiler. Water circulated at the bottom of the boiler toward the firebox, but moved away from the firebox at the water surface. Consequently, feed water was normally injected into the front end of the boiler at mid-level so that cooler water could absorb as much heat as possible from the

flues before that water reached the firebox sheets.

These variations in water temperature meant that the hotter upper flues expanded more than the cooler lower flues. This continual working of the flues caused stresses and cracking in both the flues and the flue sheets, which necessitated frequent and extensive repairs. The injected water also brought in absorbed air which accelerated corrosion of the tubes and flues.

The Interstate Commerce Commission required that all **flues** be removed from the boiler at least once every four years so that the boiler interior could be thoroughly inspected. Periods during which the engine was out of service did not count, but if five years lapsed, inspection was automatically required, though the ICC could grant extensions if circumstances warranted. The boiler was checked for corrosion, cracking, pitting or evidence of overheating. The most common area where boiler cracks would occur was at the seam where the rolled sections were joined. Any defect was repaired by a patch plate riveted in place over the crack. The ICC required that all patches be rivet repaired, not welded, but after a repaired boiler had passed ICC inspection, SP caulked the patch plate edge by welding to ensure the repair. All boilers were hydrostatic tested to a pressure 25% above normal operating pressure before being placed in service, and then at least once annually.

The **flue sheet** was most vulnerable to stress at the knuckles where it fit against the boiler shell. If a crack occurred here, the defective section could be cut out and replaced. This sectional repair was allowed twice. After two such repairs, or if the defect was behind the superheater header, which necessitated removal of the superheater unit, the entire flue sheet was replaced.

The severe thermal stress acting on the **flues** arose from the temperature variation between the front end, where incoming water was cooler, and the hotter firebox. Cracking would occur at the flue sheet end, while at the firebox end the biggest problem was burning the flue end. Defects could be repaired by "safe-ending," which consisted of welding a new 12-inch piece of flue on the tube end. This type of repair could be done twice, then the entire flue had to be replaced. The Espee countersunk and flared the flues prior to welding them

in place to obtain as much strength as possible.

There were definite schedules for frequent **boiler washes**, as determined by the locomotive class and its operating territory. Boilers had to be washed at monthly and annual ICC inspections. For AC class articulateds, GS class 4-8-4's and Mt class 4-8-2's, staybolt inspection was required every 15 days and boilers were washed then also. A locomotive receiving boiler repairs had the boiler washed down twice before being returned to service. The first wash was done prior to firing up the boiler for the steam test, and the second washing was after being blown down from the steam test. The second washing ensured all oil, cuttings, shavings, and debris were thoroughly removed.

Operating mechanical circulars officially advised crews not to "water-change" unless in an extreme emergency. If an engine was steaming badly because of foaming, it was supposed to be cooled gradually to 90°F by pumping in cooler water while one blow-down cock was partially open. When the temperature dropped to 90°F, the boiler could then be blown down and the water completely changed. The problem was that a crew out on the road usually wouldn't wait to cool the boiler

Mt-4 under construction. Note staybolt arrangement on combustion chamber and firebox and tapered cab. Note cast 4-8-2 engine bed in foreground and upside down pilot truck being worked on.

Engine 4340 in foreground undergoing repairs. Staybolts being replaced on firebox, new lagging installed. This engine has built-up frame that has been tested with whiting. Note 2-10-2 trailer truck frame on dolly.

down properly, but would blow down while filling with cool water, causing severe temperature change stresses on the boiler. Scheduled washings reduced the accumulation of boiler deposits, minimizing the occurrence of foaming and the need for water changes in service. The washings were done with hot water through washout plugs located on the boiler at the level of the crown sheet and on the backheads. Rods and scrapers were used to reach in and knock any scale loose.

Anti-foam **boiler compounds** were used to help keep water chemistry within acceptable limits. The compound was either in Nalco's NSP pulverized form to be added to the tender each time water was taken, or in the form of Nalco #79 ball compound. The chemical balls were placed directly into the boiler through the washout plugs after each wash or water change, and the 4-8-2's received three chemical balls after each washing. Each division had a set schedule governing the amount of chemical used for each class of locomotives, either in the tender or the boiler. The most severe water conditions were in desert regions, but even some

mountain divisions had water with high concentrations of minerals and silica. Passenger engines operating through Eugene, Klamath Falls, and Dunsmuir on the Shasta Route used 9 chemical balls in the boiler per run; out of Roseville and Sparks, 5 balls were used. On Arizona and New Mexico desert divisions the powder was added directly to each tank of water, usually half a pound for each 4000 to 6000 gallons, depending on the condition of the water. Around 1950, many water treatment plants were set up over the entire system to remove minerals from steam locomotive water.

Fifteen-day inspection of the **flexible staybolts** around the combustion chamber and firebox and the long stays over the crown sheet was accomplished by a man climbing into the firebox and hitting each staybolt with a hammer. He could tell by the sound if the staybolt was broken. An electrical tester was used on the hollow Flannery Tell-Tale Flexible staybolts. These flexible stays would occasionally break. As a preventative measure, the SP safety-welded staybolts on the inside of the firebox. At each scheduled class repair, three rows of staybolts were removed and replaced even though no breaks were evident. If a broken bolt was found upon inspection, the boiler jacket over the stay was removed and the staybolt replaced. The ICC required that all lagging be removed once every five years for exterior inspection of the boiler.

In 1932 the SP patented a **boiler drop plug** that was developed by F.E. Russell, Sr. as an improvement over the then-standard fusible metal plug. When the standard plug overheated due to low water on the crown sheet, the fusible metal would melt, allowing steam to blow through into the firebox, but inrushing steam would cool the fusible metal, allowing only a small opening to form. The SP's boiler drop plug had a brass button held by the fusible metal. When this melted, the button was blown out, allowing ample steam to rush in and smother the fire, preventing a boiler explosion. These plugs were installed in all engines in 1932.

The boiler appliance requiring the most repair was the **superheater**. Failure occurred in the return loop of the superheater tubes in each flue. Impurities carried over in the steam would build up hard deposits here, eventually clogging the tube, and it would blow out. These tubes were also subjected to the extreme high temperatures of the fire as they extended to within 32 inches of the combustion chamber flue sheet. In time, if they did not blow out, they would burn out. If inspection showed two or three defective tubes, the entire superheater unit was removed and replaced with a rebuilt unit. Units were rebuilt with new 18-inch sections at the return loops, and all tubing was cleaned by sanding and boring. Rebuilt units were always on hand to speed replacement. A special flatcar, with a work platform at smokebox height, was used at shops where the units were replaced. After header bolts were removed the entire superheater unit could be pulled out with a winch on the flatcar and immediately replaced with a rebuilt unit. Superheaters were always washed out through a back-wash plug at regular boiler washings.

The throttle was in the steam dome dry pipe on the Mt-1 engines, while later classes had a **front-end throttle** built into the superheater header. A cam shaft in the throttle header allowed steam to help in the movement after the throttle was once cracked open. The linkage was kept free to be easily opened and closed from the engineer's sitting position. The side-mounted Worthington **feedwater heater** was subjected to vibrations which could loosen pipe connections. No

Trailing truck, booster engine, centering rocker and pockets, flexible steam line to booster, Locomotive 4341 when new, April, 1926.

water was allowed to leak or dribble from these units under ICC safety regulations so all connections were frequently checked.

All Espee power was equipped with **front-end netting** to arrest sparks, as required by California state law, even though all SP steam power that operated there burned oil. In fact, SP used oil on all divisions except the Rio Grande and New Mexico Divisions. Many locomotives working only those divisions were equipped to burn coal, as when the SP acquired the EP&SW, it was agreed to continue use of the low-grade bituminous coal from the Dawson Field in New Mexico. The Mt-2's were built as coal burners, but the rest of the 4300s were built as and remained as oil burners.

The original netting was a modified "Master Mechanics" front end, which consisted of two vertical screens and a table plate. In 1947, the railroad conducted tests to improve the efficiency of steam locomotives at a special test plant set up at Sacramento, using GS-1 4-8-4 No. 4401. One result of the tests was a new design basket spark arrestor, cylindrical in shape and mounted between the upper flange of the nozzle stand and the lower extension of the stack. It allowed a more direct flow of gases to reduce back pressure between the firebox and smokebox, thus saving fuel. It was easier to install and maintain and was applied to most of the larger locomotive classes.

The test plant also developed an improved oil burner. The then-standard Von Boden-Ingles burner was a drooling or flat-jet type. The new Southern Pacific-patented Gyrojet **oil burner** was a gravity-fed, inside-mixing type which gave a whirling conical flame that could be controlled much better during all operating conditions. The flat jet was not as effective at high capacities. The Gyrojet was adopted in 1951 as standard and was installed on all locomotives when they came in for major shoppings.

Frames and running gear could be checked for cracks and flaws by three non-destructive means. The method used depended upon the parts involved and on the equipment available. The simplest and quickest test that could be done at almost every shop was the **whiting test**. It was used on newly finished parts or accessible parts while on the locomotive. The part was thoroughly cleaned, then a coating of kerosene or wiping oil was applied over the entire surface and allowed to remain a sufficient length of time for the oil to seep into any crack or defect. The part was then wiped dry and given a thin coating of bolted whiting (ground chalk) in water. When the whiting was dry the part was jarred with a soft, 11-lb. sledge. Any oil in a crack would stain the whiting and permit detection. After inspection, the

Worthington No. 4-BL feedwater heater and cross-compound air compressor, on 4307. F. Gillenwaters photo.

part was thoroughly cleaned again.

The whiting test was used generally for all parts until around 1932, when the **magnetic particle test**, commonly called Magnaflux, was developed. This test was adopted system-wide at all major shops by 1935 and its use was preferred when parts could be set up for this test. All paint, grease, and dirt were thoroughly cleaned off a part to be Magnafluxed. A qualified operator of the equipment carefully studied the part, then set up magnetic coils properly around it so all possible fine cracks or defects would show up regardless of direction. A powder or liquid containing fine particles of iron was placed on the part. Any crack, regardless how small, would disturb the magnetic lines of force in the test piece and the powdered iron would form a distinct line at the exact location of the defect. In the late 1940s

Worthington No. 4¼-BL feedwater heater and oil separator (bulge in large pipe), Mt-5 4373. No. 4-B heater shown on facing page. F. Gillenwaters photo.

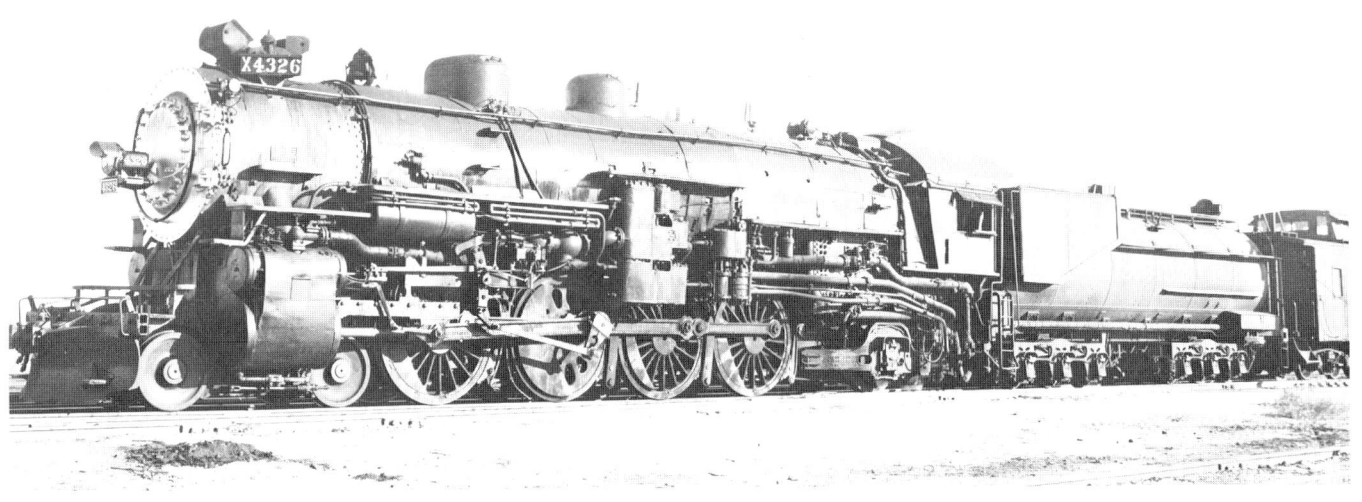

General Steel's Boxpok disc main driver has been applied to 4326. The Boxpok had small, narrow holes compared to the Universal which most Mt's received. Feedwater heater is No. 4-B. Roseville, June, 1948. A. Menke collection.

some shops were also set up to inspect mounted parts such as axles and crank pins with a third test, using ultrasonic equipment.

A whiting test of the **engine bed** was done wherever the engine was shopped for Class 1, 2, or 3 repairs. Magnaflux testing was done on parts of the engine bed or frame where the test could be satisfactorily set up. **Tires** were tested before application to the wheel centers with particular attention given to the inner surface; wheel centers were tested when applied and when removed from the engine. Main and side **rods** were tested after finishing and when removed from the engine. Bushings were pushed out all the way so the surface of the rod bore could be inspected. Pistons and **piston rods** were checked when finished and at each annual inspection, or when engines received classified repairs. On the 4-8-2, 4-8-4 and 4-10-2 type locomotives, the pistons were also inspected when the main drivers were removed from the engine. **Axles** were tested when finished, before mounting to the wheel center. Mounted axles which were hollow bored were carefully inspected for cracks, especially at the hub line and journals, by the whiting test. Hand holds on the front pilot beam of

the locomotive and end sills of tenders were Magnaflux tested at each quarterly inspection.

When the engines were shopped for Class 1, 2, and 3 repairs all **spring rigging** including spring saddles was removed and annealed, then inspected for flaws, cracks, and worn surfaces. At Class 4 and 5 shoppings the spring rigging was checked in place and any part reaching the limit of wear was renewed or repaired.

The **main driver** received the piston thrust along with the reciprocating forces of the side rods. If a cracked spoke occurred, it was usually on the main driver. In 1946, it became standard practice to replace defective main drivers with "Boxpok" (General Steel Castings) or "Universal" (Locomotive Finished Materials) **disc wheel centers** which were much more durable. But spoked main drivers were only replaced if flawed, so many locomotives retained all spoked drivers until they were scrapped. Reciprocating forces on the drivers caused them to wear to a slightly elliptical shape, so wheels were always measured when a tire was removed. Any discrepancy, even a few hundredths of an inch, was built up by welding and the wheel re-turned.

The alligator **crosshead guides** presented some

Large holes typify Universal disc main driver. Tender is 120-C-6. San Francisco, Sept. 24, 1956. D. Richter photo.

Engine 4369 on Lidgerwood track at West Oakland. Workman adjusts cutter head on brake hanger. Note cable to Lidgerwood engine on front coupler, and air hose connections. Feb. 1949. B.W. Griffiths photo, Menke collection.

SCHEDULE OF MILES RUN AND MINIMUM MILEAGE BETWEEN CLASSIFIED REPAIRS
(Excluding Lidgerwood)
Period twelve months ended Dec. 31, 1949

Class of Locomotives 4-8-2
Minimum Schedule 150,000
Number of Locomotives Repaired 41
Average Mileage 127,000

DETAILS BY DIVISION ASSIGNMENT

Division	No. Locos. Repaired	Avg. Mileage
Western	12	132,000
Sacramento	7	109,000
Salt Lake	9	138,000
Shasta	1	62,000
Portland	1	169,000
Coast	4	130,000
Los Angeles	4	111,000
Tucson	1	157,000
Rio Grande	2	139,000

maintenance problems. Flanges would wear, and if not corrected, the resulting play caused pounding which would bow the guide. The Espee cast replacement shoes to exact size and did not machine them before installation. Around 1947, the road started applying multiple-bearing guides and crossheads to some of its own Mt's. The EP&SW Mt-2's were originally built with this type guide. Multiple-bearing guides were very

Multiple-bearing crosshead guide and Nathan mechanical lubricator. F. Gillenwaters photo.

dependable and easy to maintain, but steam operations ended before very many Mt's were so equipped. Some engines of each class did receive them.

Locomotives assigned to run over mountain districts would show excessive **flange wear** much sooner than engines used elsewhere. The Shasta Division's severe curvature necessitated 30-day tire turnings on road engines, while Sacramento Division power would need tire turning in 45 to 50 days. Tire and flange wear was checked at each monthly inspection. When it was noted that the driving tires would require changing within the next 90 days, the locomotive was scheduled for a tire change. To replace a tire, the wheel was usually dropped and the tire removed, though if a fast job was needed, the engine could be jacked up and the tire heated in place and removed.

If the tires could be turned and contoured and still be within ICC limits as to thickness, the job could be done without removing them from the locomotive. The major shops, Roseville, Sparks, Oakland, Eugene, Taylor, Bayshore, and El Paso, had Lidgerwood tire-turning facilities. This was a straight track section over

Lidgerwood winch. Note cable, blocking, old F-50-2 flat car. Oakland, Feb. 1949. B.W. Griffiths photo, Menke collection.

which the locomotive was pulled with a cable by a stationary engine, the Lidgerwood. All the running gear and brake rigging was cleaned thoroughly, brake heads on the drivers were removed, and cutter heads applied to the brake hangers. The tender brakes were left to brake the engine. Air from either the engine or a ground hose actuated the brake-cutter heads. The engine was pulled toward the Lidgerwood at 15 to 17 ft. per minute with a brake pressure of 10 to 20 pounds.

Spring-pad lubricators were repaired or repadded at Sacramento, Los Angeles and El Paso. Repadding only was done at West Oakland and Mission Bay. All metal work for these pads was manufactured at Sacramento and shipped to all the other shops.

The **power reverse** gear was maintained to respond to a change of one notch on the reverse quadrant. It was subject to vibration and its mounts were inspected to ensure secure fastenings. At Class 3 and heavier repairs, reverse gear was dismantled, cleaned, checked and re-

Cracked frame prepared for welding.

set. The reverse lever rod was 1-inch extra-strong iron pipe and was kept as straight as possible.

The **pistons** and cylinders were subjected to temperatures as high as 750°F. The primary factor was friction, either from piston travel while working heavily at low speed, or from high-speed operation. At 60 miles per hour, the piston traveled more than 1300 ft. per minute. The steel in the piston would turn blue from high temperatures, but was not detrimentally affected, and replacement was rare. Extreme temperatures would eventually burn out the piston rings; both rings and packing had to be replaced periodically. The cylinders themselves rarely had to be rebored because of heat damage. **Drifting valves** which released back pressure helped reduce friction when the locomotive was coming downgrade.

The built-up **frame** was more subject to cracks than the cast engine bed. Flaws were sought with the whiting test, or Magnaflux where this test could be set up. Cracks in the cast engine bed usually occurred where the cylinder saddle was attached. Such cracks in the casting were cut out and weld repaired.

Other components such as injectors, boiler check valves, lubricators, air pump, and cab appliances all required maintenance. These and fittings for the steam, oil, air and water lines were all checked periodically.

In the days when steam reigned supreme, shops maintained locomotives in like-new condition. Modernization sent engines out of the backshop better than when originally built. In those years, the shop men would take great pride in their responsibility, and a well-deserved pride it was when a locomotive rolled out, sparkling in new paint, its exhaust cracking in a syncopation of perfection. ■

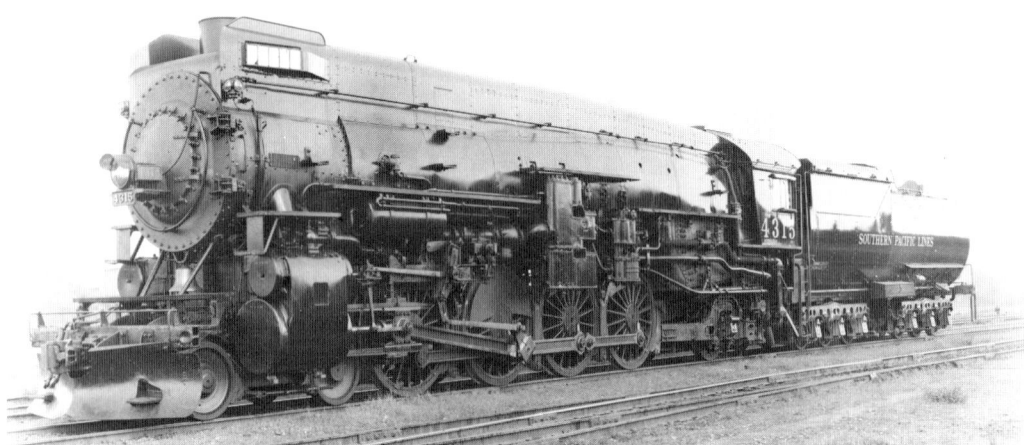

Above – Engine 4361 was the first Mt to receive "Daylight" paint on May 23, 1946, just prior to when "Lines" was omitted in June, 1946. Note small 9" lettering in the orange color stripe, not in upper red stripe as on the 4-8-4's. When the remaining four Mt's were painted "Daylight" the 20" tender lettering was used. See page 92 for color view.

Middle – Two views of 4315, the first to receive the skyline casing on February 1, 1939.

Below – Two top views of skyline casing and smoke deflector. F. Gillenwaters photos.

Above – View of 4320 clearly shows the Universal disc main driver with its large triangular holes. Note the rebuilt "sport" cab, covering over sand pipe valves and pressed steel pilot. The tender is Class 120-C-5. G. M. Best photo, Los Angeles, Sept. 27, 1949. Arnold Menke collection.

Below – Mt-4 No.4363 at Oakland in 1941. Snow pilot suggests that this engine operated on the mountain districts of the Shasta or Overland Routes. Of particular interest is the disc type apparatus at the bottom of the bell. Arnold Menke supplied this photo and states that several other 4-8-2's had this application, but he doesn't know why. Speculation 1: If these engines operated in snow conditions, this may have been a shield to keep blowing snow from freezing up the air ringer mechanism in the bell. Speculation 2: It may have been a sound muffler due to some local noise restriction ordinance where the engine operated.

Above – Three views of Mt-4 4365 show changes over the years. At Sacramento in 1938, the engine sports an interesting paint scheme, with the smokebox, stack and firebox done in silver. This is 8 years before it became standard practice in 1946 to paint all smokebox fronts silver. Most probably this engine was assigned to the *Forty-Niner* (see page 125), and thus received special treatment. The indicator appears ready to receive a two-digit train number (possibly "49"). D.L. Joslyn photo, A. Menke collection.

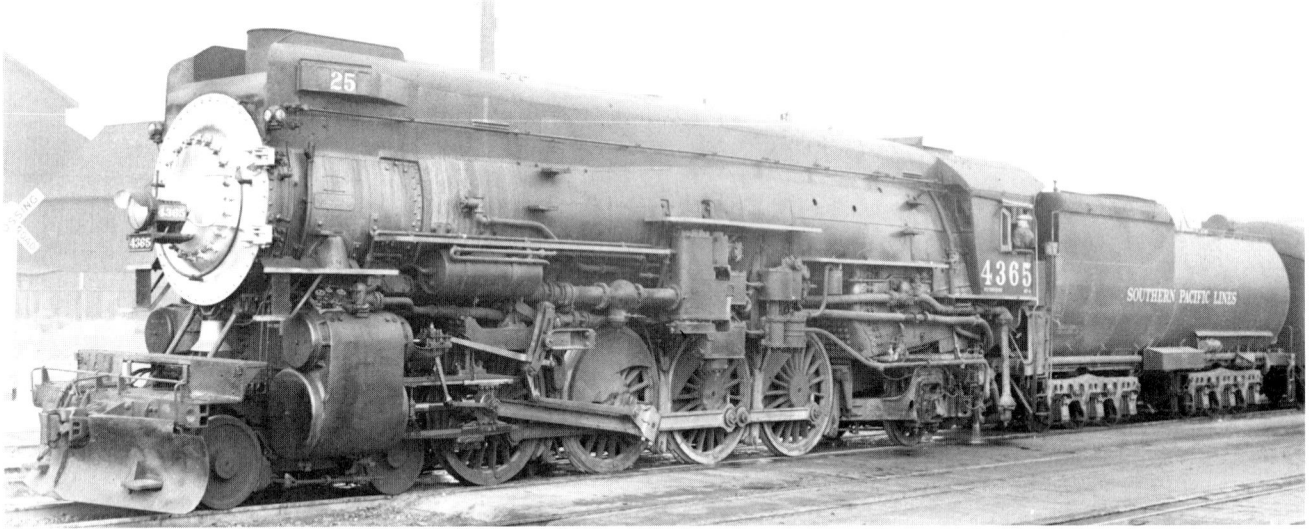

Above – By 1940 the engine had received the skyline casing. Note the original forward location of the train indicators and bell below the smokebox. No. 25, "Passenger," seen at Oakland, was the local Oakland-Sparks train.
Below – 1946 view shows 4365 has received the Boxpok main driver, one of only a few Mt's that got this type disc driver, as most received the Universal driver. Train 19 was the Oakland-Portland *Klamath*. Both, R. McFarland photos, Arnold Menke collection.

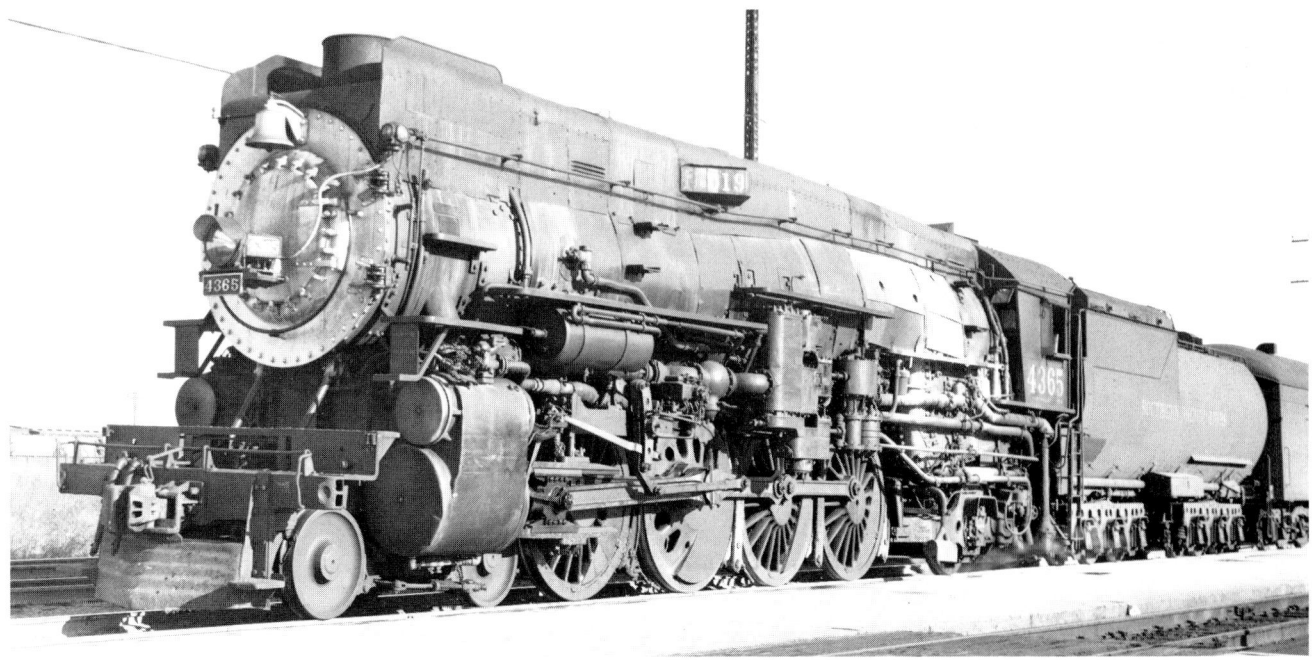

Right – The painters doing 4357 even left the headlight silver! They did trim the smokebox door hinges in black. Undoubtedly someone expressing his individualism! This was not common, but in the period the *Forty-Niner* ran, engines assigned to it did get the "little extra" treatment. Berkeley, 1938. R. McFarland photo, A. Menke collection.

Below – This beautiful view of freshly shopped 4352 clearly shows the special blue-green paint scheme on the boiler and cylinder jackets. (See text on the following page.) Extra treatment also included an all-silver smokebox and stack (at this time it was usually graphite), white striping on the running boards and tires, and nickel cylinder covers. Sacramento, circa 1930. A. Menke collection.

Above – This HO model of 4328 represents a paint scheme used on a number of locomotives assigned to passenger service in the 1920s. It clearly shows in black and white photographs (below and right). It was also used on 4-4-2's, 4-6-0's, 4-6-2's, and even 2-8-2's and 2-10-2's working passenger trains on mountain districts. It had disappeared by the early 1930s, and had no Common Standard paint drift panel. Model paint colors are based on recollections of railroad men who had seen them. See text below.

Floquil Model Railroad paints were mixed as follows:

Blue-green (boiler jacket, cylinder and air pump wrappers
    6 parts R38 GN Gray-Green
    1 part R56 GN Big Sky Blue

Red-brown (cab roof)
    2 parts DH10 Caboose Red,
    1 part R25 Tuscan Red

SP Graphite (smokebox front and side, firebox)
    3 parts R100 Old Silver,
    1 part R119 Graphite

Lettering – Synthetic Gray enamel, decals from California Locomotive Works

Colored Boiler Jackets

I N THE FIRST EDITION of this book the definite differences in color of the boiler jacket and cylinder covers on some engines were pointed out. Tone and opaqueness led to the conclusion that it was definitely a paint application on those engines. Unfortunately, when this practice was current, from the late "teens" to the early 1930s, there was no color photography. But this conclusion was corroborated by interviews with photographers Al Phelps and Wil Whittaker, and SP Boiler Inspector at Bayshore Shops, Frank Longo. All stated that they definitely remembered seeing the painted treatment done on some engines, most often those used in passenger service. But they also stated that on other engines the color hue difference was due to the material used on the jacket of that engine, and the luster and color came from the sheet metal itself.

The presentation tweaked the attention of many, and it brought about some fine research and documentation of the materials used by the Central Pacific and SP for jackets, and also in regards to the painted jackets.

Robert A. Pecotich, co-author of *Southern Pacific Steam Pictorial – Volume I* (see References), wrote an appendix to that book giving an excellent review of "Russia Iron" and later "America Iron" that was used for locomotive boiler jackets. He also analyzed how different black and white film emulsions and sunlight conditions could influence the images of those jacket materials preserved in photographic prints.

Russia Iron was first produced in the early 1800s by factories in the Ural Mountains. It was initially used for non-railroad purposes, such as roofing material. The process heated iron sheets with charcoal in the near-absence of oxygen. This procedure, combined with at least three cycles of trip-hammering or "planishing" and additional, oxygen-deprived reheating, created a unique sheet metal. Though more expensive, it was extremely rust resistant, even at high temperatures and even after being rolled. The purity of the sheet iron, temperature differences, duration of hammering, and the amount of oxygen present all influenced the hue variations. Sheets were graded as to the quality of the finish and were further sorted by color. The different grades gave a wide diversity of color, ranging from very

Above – This freshly shopped P-5 class 4-6-2 has "LA 12-24-22" stenciled on the cylinder cover. It clearly shows the painted blue-green paint on the jacket and cylinder cover. Workmen are doing a final steam check. The man atop the boiler behind the turret is setting the "pops." Note the steam turret cover is off and the pressure gauge is attached to the roundhouse steam hookup valve. This was an extremely ear-shattering job! The first safety valve released a pound or so above normal operating pressure, the second at six to eight pounds higher. T. Taber photo, A. Menke collection.

light blue or silver to very dark blue, to various gray and gray-green hues, or even umber red to magenta.

Locomotive builders in the United States started using Russia Iron for boiler jacket application about 1845. Its characteristic gloss was maintained by wiping the surface with refined oil, which added to its warm luster and tone.

In 1885, a process for iron sheet similar to Russia Iron was developed in Pennsylvania. This sheeting was called "America Iron," and it was soon utilized by many railroads, especially after 1900 when Russia Iron became prohibitively expensive. The SP did have this jacketing applied to some of its locomotives, including Mt-1 No. 4300. Concurrently, newer heat-resistant paints were also being developed. Evidence clearly shows that just after World War I, for economic reasons, the SP also began painting the boiler and cylinder jackets of some engines to match the distinctive blue-green or gray-green metal color hues of Russia or

Below – 1906 Baldwin-built Class A-3 engine shows off what is probably a jacket of "America Iron." Note how the luster is more translucent, coming from the metal sheeting itself.

America Iron. It was primarily done on locomotives used in passenger service. The practice was discontinued in the early 1930s, probably due to the Depression.

There was never a Common Standard paint mix for the blue-green color. I was told that the mix was done by each shop, so engines from different shops could well have a different tone and hue. Any special paint job was authorized by the Master Mechanic on a "time available" basis. Each painter used a set of standard colors-in-oil which he would mix to his satisfaction. Colors were mixed until a desired shade of blue-green or gray-green that "looked right" to the painter's eye was achieved. Thus there occurred many variations on individual engines over the years.

When SP 4-6-2 No. 2472 was being restored, a blue-green paint was found under layers of black paint on injector piping alongside the boiler. They also found red paint on the cab roof that matched SP "Seat and Sash Paint," color drift panel No. 133, Specification No. SP 148. There is no doubt that between around 1918 and 1933 numerous locomotives did have the special paint scheme.

In the early 1940s the painted jacket again appeared, but this time only on a few passenger terminal switchers. West Oakland shop men state that they painted No. 1270 using SP "Machinery Green" enamel, color drift panel No. 144, Specification No. SP 241. E.R. Mohr recalls that when the engine was wiped down with "wiping oil" and later simply lantern oil, it took on a warmer and darker tone with an amber cast. ■

Above – A dethroned queen, 4356, sits alongside the dowager of the passenger diesel fleet, the 6011. The E2-A was the oldest diesel on the SP, and affectionately became known as the "Queen Mary." A one-of-a-kind on the roster, the Winton-engined unit was built in 1937 as the cab engine for the *City of San Francisco*, and first operated under joint C&NW, UP, and SP ownership. In 1948 the SP took over ownership, and it continued to operated for over a year on the Overland Route, usually hauling the "Mail Train." It later became No. 6017, and Los Angeles Shops rebuilt and re-engined her to E7-A specifications, outshopping the renewed unit in February, 1954. She was retired on July 26, 1966, outlasting the adjacent 4-8-2 by 12 years. Ogden, August, 1949. Guy Dunscomb photo.

Below – Late in its life, 4303 has been relegated to local service operating around Reno-Sparks. Here the entire consist is an SP ballast hopper, a PFE reefer, and a steel cupola caboose. September, 1954. R.R. Wallin collection.

Above – Freshly shopped 4337 moves off the turntable at Mission Bay Roundhouse, to run over to Third and Townsend for morning commute service. Though the tenders of four GS-class locomotives are visible, time is running out for steam, and a lone diesel intruder (E7-A 6000) sits on a garden track. Still, it is gratifying to see a locomotive at this time in such pristine condition. Stan Kistler photo, July 18, 1955.

Below – Engine 4340 rests at Fresno Yard in the company of F-4 class 2-10-2 3680 (only its 16,000-gallon Vanderbilt tender is visible at center) and at the left, bracketing the oil and water columns, a pair of 0-6-0 switchers. On the left is 1299, an S-8 class engine which was transferred from subsidiary Arizona Eastern in 1924 (it formerly was AE 40), and to its right is 1260, one of SP's Sacramento-built S-12 class. The date is May 28, 1955, and the end of steam is very near. Stan Kistler photo.

Left – Engine 4360's exhaust blast rattles the windows of the Fourth St. tower as commute train No. 122 leaves San Francisco in 1956. The Mt's were preferred by engineers for this service, even compared to GS engines, because of their excellent acceleration. Donald Duke photo.

Below – At South San Francisco, the first Mt, No. 4300, leads a late-afternoon commuter train toward the Peninsula in September, 1954. In this era, at least 20 such trains arrived in San Francisco each workday morning, and a similar number departed for south Peninsula points every afternoon. Jim Seagrave collection.

Above – Train Nos. 5-6 was the *Argonaut*, a standard heavyweight sleeper and chair car train that operated between New Orleans and Los Angeles, routed via Phoenix on the Sunset Route. It usually got hand-me-down equipment from the *Sunset Limited*, which was streamlined by this time. Here we see the westbound train, powered by an Mt-4, taking on water. The use of steam on this train is nearing its end, and the 4354 is showing the wear and tear of deferred cosmetic maintenance. R.R. Wallin collection.

Below – A timeless scene in steam days of a father showing his son how it's done. The commute trains approached stations at speed, stopped on a dime, and were on their way within one minute. As this photo demonstrates, the Pacifics which received skyline casings had a resemblance to the Mt's; this is P-10 2491 on train 116. From today's perspective, the automobiles are nearly as interesting as the locomotive and train. Taken at Hillsdale, Calif., by Jack Whitmeyer in 1952.

Above – Many thought the Mt-2's were not as pretty as the SP engines. Perhaps it was the centered headlight, the higher front of the skyline casing needed to cover the Elesco feedwater heater, or the squarish cab and tender that kept them from having that true "SP appearance." The 4390 had a lower headlight, and it did "look" better (see p. 62). Note in this 1948 Sacramento Shops photo that there are already old AC-class 2-8-8-2's sitting in storage. Guy Dunscomb photo.

Below – No "pretty engine" here. No. 4335 was in a roll-over accident and shows the results. It is interesting to see this view of the skyline casing. Note that this locomotive also has the special apparatus in the bell (see page 75). The drivers in the background appear to be coated for a whiting test. D. Joslyn photo, Sacramento, November 24, 1940. A. Menke collection.

Above – Engine 4333 and train No. 17, the all-Pullman *Cascade* in pre-air conditioned days, are seen drifting downgrade near Azalea with Mt. Shasta dominating the background. R. Church collection, circa 1930.

Below – Crescent Lake, Oregon is a water stop for the second section of the *Klamath*. The reason for the special was not noted, but it consisted of an express reefer, two coaches, a diner and three Pullman cars. Twelve-wheeler 2938 simmers near the enginehouse in the background. Al Phelps photo, June, 1951.

Left – Reflections on a passing train. Lower quadrant semaphores hold the "Coast Mail," No. 72, headed by 4302, in the siding at Concepcion for the westward *Daylight*, holding timetable speed at 55 mph due to curvature. Photo by John Illman, March 18, 1951.

Below – A classic Otto Perry view of the "Coast Mail" in earlier times, slowing for the depot at San Luis Obispo in July, 1937 behind Mt-4 4357 and 4-6-0 2376. In later years, the grove of eucalyptus trees behind the train would grow considerably, and a new depot, built in 1942, would stand just behind the place Perry stood to get this shot. Neg. 16001, Denver Public Library.

Richard Steinheimer

The Departure

Tᴀᴀɪɴ ᴛɪᴍᴇ at the Oakland Mole for "52," the *San Joaquin Daylight*. Such sights and sounds, once witnessed, are unforgettable. The engineer checks his timepiece and leans out to watch the conductor as the last patrons hurriedly board. The fireman adjusts his firing valve and keeps a light blower going to maintain the boiler pressure "on the mark." The steam turbo-generator whines, and there is the occasional pulsation of the air compressor. Dwarf semaphore signals show green for the aligned tracks ahead.

Moments before the scheduled departure time, the action begins. The release of the automatic train brake is marked by a hiss of air below the cab from the distributor valve, and the air pump jumps into action to restore the main reservoir pressure. Next comes the hiss/ka-chunk as the engineer moves the power reverse

gear forward into the "corner," for maximum power.

"Boooard," and the car attendants pick up the footsteps and swing aboard. The sounds of closing traps and latching double doors echo the length of the train. A final look up and down the consist by the conductor. It's 6:50 AM and he turns forward and waves "highball." Then the beauty of steam and a man in complete control begins, a ballet of machine and master.

On goes the headlight. Two short blasts of the whistle; the air ringer starts in the bell. The left hand flips off the independent engine brake with a hiss, and both hands reach up for a finesse opening of the throttle, just enough steam to gain almost imperceptible motion. A deep-throated shwoosh of the first exhaust. Movement, and the engineer opens a little more throttle, again just enough to achieve full smooth power without drivers slipping or a surging action.

Now the exhaust is barking sharply as the big 4-8-2

Richard Steinheimer

leans into her task. A quick look back to check the train; everything is all right. Looking forward the engineer gives his high-stepper a few more notches on the throttle and sits back, arm on the rest as the engine blasts by. This is a seasoned and skillful "engineer," not a "hogger." He is underway, and he is in command. That white Kromer hat identifies a veteran of experience, position and seniority. Exhaust noise gives way to the cushioned clickity-clack of accelerating cars. As the round-end parlor observation slips by one wonders how that much speed could be gained in such a short distance. Next train out, the *Shasta Daylight*, but the PA's won't put on a show like this!

No one could better capture departure time than did Richard Steinheimer in this beautiful and artful triptych done in 1950. One artist capturing another artist in a moment of time. ■

Above – Mt-1 4308 has just switched out a cut of cars and is backing to the water plug as a westbound freight clears the station. Modesto's "Dependable" truck dealer seems to have a lot full of pickups awaiting buyers. Guy Dunscomb photo, August, 1953.

Below – As steam was ending its days, the Valley became a last stronghold. By this time most passenger trains were handled by diesel power, so many 4-8-2 and 4-8-4 locomotives were kept earning revenue by hauling freight. Here a 40-car westbound leaves Bakersfield on April 21, 1955. Henry R. Griffiths, Jr. photo.

Above – On August 12, 1939, near Harney, Nevada, the Overland Route's flagship, the streamlined *City of San Francisco*, was derailed by an act of sabotage. The railroad had to use conventional equipment to substitute for the damaged train. Here we see 4335 awaiting departure from the 16th Street Station in Oakland with No. 102, the eastbound makeshift *City*. The thirteen-car train is all heavyweight except for two cars. James E. Boynton photo. August 14, 1939.

Below – Doubleheading "Daylight"-painted Mt's, led by 4352, charge the Tehachapi grade south of Bakersfield between Edison and Sandcut. By the time No. 52 reaches the loop at Caliente their speed will be cut by one-half, and they both will be knuckling down into the 27-mile climb to Summit, just beyond Tehachapi. Guy Dunscomb photo, March 27, 1948.

A beautiful portrait of No. 52, the *San Joaquin Daylight*, working southbound up the Tehachapi grade. Point engine 4352 and road engine 4353 are both in the "Daylight" paint scheme. Photo taken by R.G. Denechaud in the summer of 1946, courtesy Guy C. Denechaud.

Operations

The *Lark* awaits departure at San Francisco.

THE ESPEE 4300s could well have been designated the railroad's general service locomotives. These lanky 4-8-2's proved in service to have just the right combination of technology to allow high-stepping grace at the head of a string of varnish, or the gutsy brawn to knuckle down and walk away with a heavy tonnage freight. The big engines were a favorite of roundhouse dispatchers and crews alike, for their dependability, on any assignment whatever, was beyond reproach. Their 73-inch drivers gave them a versatility not surpassed even by their later GS-class stablemates.

The Northerns, especially the 80-inch GS-3, -4 and -5's, were ideally suited for high-wheeling the new streamliners which they were designed to haul, but the large drivers caused them to be somewhat slippery. Engineers preferred an Mt to a GS for a given train, because the Mt could dig in and start without slipping on a heavy train that could cause a GS to lose her feet. The GS classification of the 4-8-4's originally stood for "Golden State." In the war year of 1942, the War Production Board would not consider using scarce materials to build strictly a passenger engine. When the SP asked to have the GS-6 class built, officials stated to the WPB that GS designated "General Service" and that the new 4-8-4's were to be used in freight service also. Thus, the 4-8-4's acquired the "General Service" title more by a turn of fate, than by the fact that they were any more suited to it than the 4-8-2's. The GS's were

The combined *San Francisco* and *Overland Limiteds*, as described in the text below. Regular consists were 12 headend cars, 1 club car, 4 Pullmans, and 1 Pullman observation. Shown here leaving Battle Mountain, Nevada: arrival, 3:17 PM, departure, 3:20 PM – On time! July 11, 1938. Al Phelps photo.

outstanding engines in their own right, but it was a fact that crews had no preference for them over the Mt's.

It is easy to see the feeling of the respect the crews had for 4300s after one has talked to engineers and firemen who had the good fortune to hold down a seat box on one of the Mountains. That feeling could be heard in the voice of the engineer who recalled running "27" in the Depression years, an Mt on the point, and a 22-car heavyweight train behind the tender. No. 27 was the combined *San Francisco Limited* and *Overland Limited*, and 22 cars were its regular duty. This consist probably made it one of the longest trains in the country on a daily basis. One 4300 could keep this train "on the advertised," with the only westbound helper district required in Nevada being over the Pequop Mountains from Montello to the summit at Valley Pass. The train was split at Sparks, Nev., and ran separately as No. 9 and No. 27 over the Sierra and on into Oakland.

A gleam came into the old veteran's eyes as he told of "taking right off" going west out of Battle Mountain, Nev., using the booster for a smooth and slipless start. How, by the time he was only 4 miles out of town he was doing better than 60 miles per hour and accelerating right past a railfan photographer in a Model A Ford futilely attempting to pace the train on the adjacent highway. In the winter months, two Mt's were used on this train, not for power, but so the second engine could supply sufficient steam to heat the long train!

On their original territory, the Sunset Route, they soon gained the admiration of the crews, who knew that Mt's could be coaxed beyond their theoretical limits to keep name trains on time, or get them back onto time if necessary. Fireman Al Phelps recalls one specific time in 1947 when engine 4324 and No. 43, the *Californian*, were an hour late out of El Paso. The El Paso to Lordsburg crew, and his engineer from Lordsburg to Tucson, a 312-mile distance, "worked the big girl for everything she was worth," and No. 43 arrived in Tucson on time. In those days there was no "hedging" time in schedules; the hour was made up by sheer running.

A most creditable achievement in the operating annals of the 4300s came between July 11th and 19th in 1936. Nearly 10,000 Shriners, Elks and dental delegates traveled the SP to Portland and on to Seattle for conventions. Right in the middle of heavy summer tourist travel, this monumental movement involved handling 21 special trains northbound and 14 southbound. In addition, there were numerous chartered car parties on the regular trains, many of which ran in extra sections. As all train movements, both regular and special, were exceedingly heavy, it was necessary to borrow from the Tucson, Los Angeles, Coast and Salt Lake Divisions, 14 of the powerful 4-8-2 passenger engines to augment the power already assigned to the Portland, Shasta, Sac-

Locomotive 4324 champs at the bit to leave Bowie, Arizona, and make up time on the *Californian*, running late this day. Ten-wheeler 2105 stands with connecting local No. 381, while the cab-forward at left is in the hole with an eastbound extra. December 14, 1947. Al Phelps photo.

ramento and Western Divisions, in moving the trains between Oakland and Portland.

It was also necessary to establish 12 additional telegraph shifts to handle train orders for all these extra movements. The operator at Arbuckle, located between Davis and Gerber in the Sacramento Valley on the "Westside" line, remembers well the night of July 11. Train No. 20, the northbound *Klamath*, ran in 10 sections. Each train was headed by a 4300. When the headlight and green markers showed in the distance, the operator would "wink" the order board (raise the semaphore arm up and down so the lights winked). This signaled the engineer that "19" orders were to be picked up. ("19" orders were picked up on the fly; a "31" order had to be signed for, thus the train stopped.) As the train slowed to 50 miles per hour, the fireman would cross the cab, reach out and pick up the orders from a hoop held up by the operator. Then the exhaust would bark loudly as the engineer opened up and the train rushed off, the rear markers quickly disappearing into the darkness.

At Dunsmuir the engine facilities were humming all night long, for at that time, it was standard practice to change motive power there. A 4300 was waiting to take over the first section when it arrived. The first section's engine was then serviced and it took over the second section. Engines were dropped back like this for all sec-

tions, and thus no time was lost in servicing. Helper engines were also added to the point at Dunsmuir for the steep climb to Black Butte and Grass Lake. Mechanics were stationed at intermediate points ready to make emergency repairs to engines or cars, though their services were little required. Likewise, spare locomotives held under steam at strategic points, ready to leave on a moment's notice, were not called upon. There was a total of 74 train movements of all classes into and out of Oakland's 3rd Street terminal on July 11, and 76 movements into the terminal on July 18. The entire operation was an exceptional performance by the men of the railroad and their equipment.

In June, 1950, another interesting event was added to the 4300 history. The Shriners met in Los Angeles and again the SP, along with Santa Fe and Union Pacific, was responsible for the monumental movement of 200,000 joy-bent delegates. Mission Tower moved 80 specials inbound and 77 outbound at Los Angeles Union Passenger Terminal. The UP used four-unit freight diesels on their specials, but SP and Santa Fe used steam. Espee brought in GS-6 4-8-4's to help a number of 4300s assigned to the specials, as Southern Pacific handled the greatest number of trains into the city. Six of the specials came from El Paso, 16 came via the Coast Route, and 17 from the San Joaquin Division.

A railroad city on wheels, appropriately named "Fez

Typical appearance of locomotives operating on the "Northern District" (lines north of San Francisco) at the time of the convention specials in 1936 on the Shasta Route. Box on pilot deck was for a fire hose. Train No. 7 is the *Shasta.* Fairfield, August, 1937. Al Phelps photo.

City," was strung along SP's River Station yards, known to Espee men as "the cornfield." Eleven complete trains made up of Pullman cars, diners, and supply cars were steam heated by Mt's 4305, 4312, and 4321, serving as stationary boilers. When the convention was over these engines were assigned to power outbound specials. Santa Fe and UP also had "Fez Cities," the UP's 45 cars heated with two auxiliary steam-generating cars and two 0-6-0's. The Santa Fe used Mountains Nos. 3747 and 3713 to heat their trains.

An unexpected duty pulled on occasion by 4300s was local service. When any engine was outshopped with new bearings throughout, it had to run at slow speeds for several hundred miles until the bearings were broken in and did not run hot. Speed was limited to about 25 miles per hour and quite often the break-in period was spent helping slow freights. Some branch lines had heavier rail and on occasion, especially during World War II, a 4-8-2 would work locals to break in. Taylor Roundhouse would regularly send larger engines to work the Santa Paula branch, where trains

were fairly long. The branch was the original main line on the Coast (until 1904 when the line through Chatsworth was completed), and had heavier rails. Even the resplendent 4334, with raised brass cab numbers and tender letters, gave a touch of class to the Fillmore local in 1943, breaking in after receiving new bearings at Los Angeles Shops.

These are but a few instances in the operating annals of the Mt's, demonstrating their capability to take on any assignment the engine dispatcher deemed necessary and handle it with ease, while showing the outstanding dependability that gave a deserved sense of pride to officials at 65 Market Street.

The variations of climate, geography, and traffic over lines extending from Portland to Ogden, to Los Angeles and New Orleans, called for varied operating procedures across SP's broad rail network. It was in the 1930s that the 4300s reigned supreme, and it is of interest to see the train assignments of these locomotives, and the special conditions on the various routes. ∎

How many would envy the chance to have held down this engineer's seatbox? Not one crewman who was talked to, thought anything but the best of the 4300s, especially the SP engines. The ex-EP&SW versions did ride rougher because the cab was higher and equalization differed. Reputation of the SP 4300s was that they fired the easiest of any class, the boiler responding immediately to a change of one notch on the throttle. Roseville, May, 1948. Guy Dunscomb photo.

Mt Class Locomotive Assignments
January 31, 1936

Salt Lake Division (124)
4313 4333 4334 4335 4337
4338 4339 4343 4359 4363
4364 4365 4366 4367 4368
4369 4370 4371 4372 4373
4374 4375 4376

Los Angeles Division (155)
4301 4314 4315 4316 4317
4318 4319 4320 4321 4322
4330

Coast Division (182)
4323 4324 4325 4326 4351
4352 4353 4354 4355 4356
4357 4362

Western Division (225)
4328 4332

San Joaquin Division (102)
4327

Shasta District (79)
(Part of Sacto. Div.)
4340 4341 4342 4344

Portland Division (139)
4329 4331 4345 4346 4347
4348

Sacramento Division (145)
4336 4340 4341 4342 4344
4349 4350

Rio Grande Division (109)
4300 4302 4303 4304 4305
4358 4360 4361 4385 4386
4387 4388 4389 4390

Tucson Division (114)
4306 4307 4308 4309 4310
4311 4312

( ) indicates number of steam engines assigned that division.
Total engines on roster in revenue service: 1404

4303 taking on sand, oil checked, at Los Angeles, April, 1924. A. Menke collection.

Mt Class Locomotive Assignments
December 31, 1948

Western Division (236)
4303	4310	4315	4318	4323
4327	4334	4336	4338	4339
4341	4345	4346	4348	4350
4351	4357	4360	4361	4362
4363	4365	4366	4367	4370
4374				

Salt Lake Division (113)
4300	4316	4320	4322	4329
4330	4332	4333	4347	4371
4372	4375			

Coast Division (161)
4305	4307	4311	4324	4343
4355	4368	4369		

Sacramento Division (131)
4326	4328	4331	4344	4349
4359	4385	4386	4387	4388
4389	4390			

Shasta Division (113)
4319	4321

Portland Division (190)
4306	4309	4313	4314	4325
4342	4356	4358	4376	

San Joaquin Division (82)
4373

Los Angeles Division (173)
4312	4352	4353	4354	4364

Tucson Division (105)
4308	4317

Rio Grande Division (84)
4301	4302	4304	4335	4337
4340				

( ) indicates number of steam engines assigned that division.
Total engines on roster in revenue service
Steam: 1388, D.E. Switch 123, D.E. Rd. Switch 3, D.E. Pass. 9, D.E. F. T. 28

It is interesting to note where the Mt's were assigned when they were the primary passenger power, and compare the reassignments when the 4400's came along.

4349 rides the turntable at Dunsmuir, July, 1937. Guy Dunscomb photo.

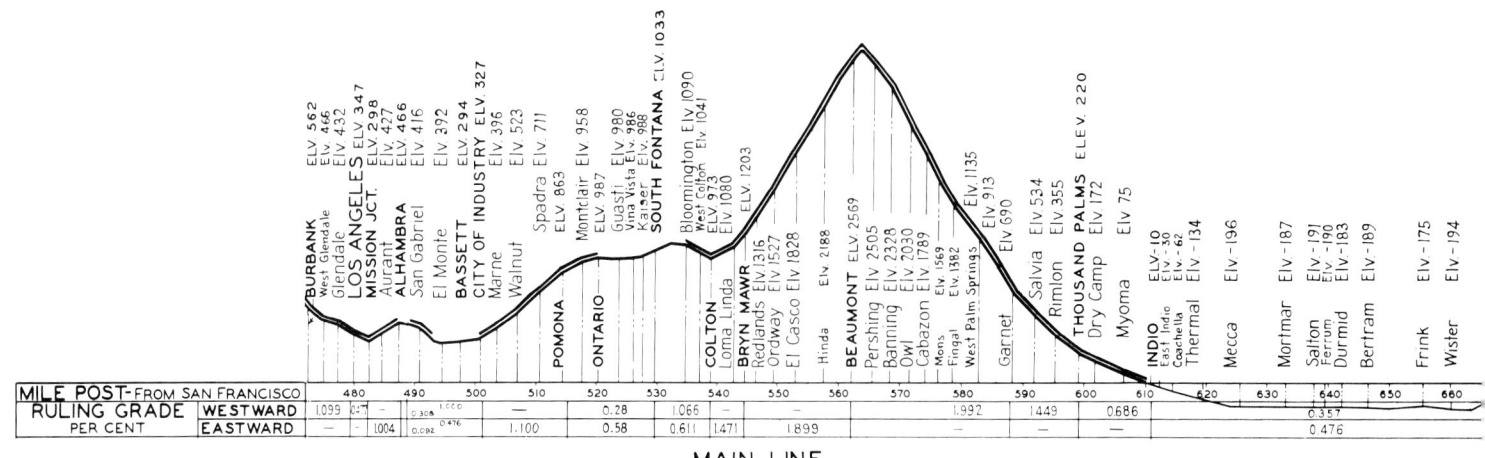

MAIN LINE
SAN FRANCISCO TO EL PASO
Via Valley and North Lines
PART 2 BAKERSFIELD TO NILAND. CALIF.

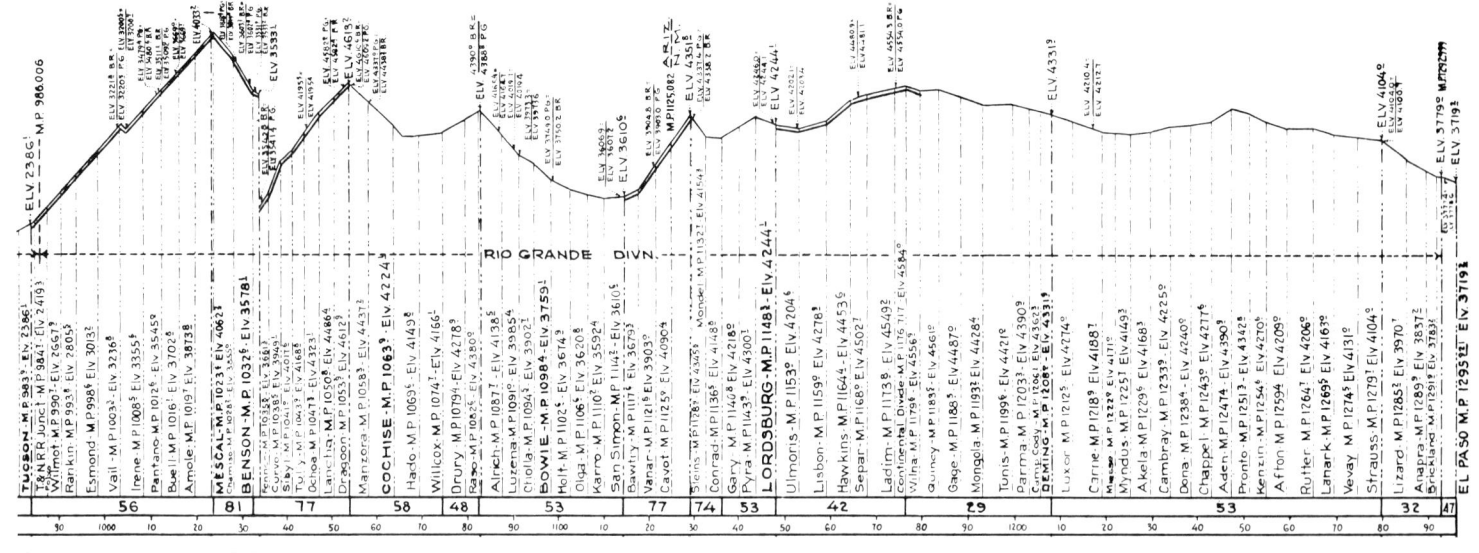

MAIN LINE
SAN FRANCISCO TO EL PASO
VIA VALLEY AND NORTH LINES
PART 3 - MARICOPA TO EL PASO

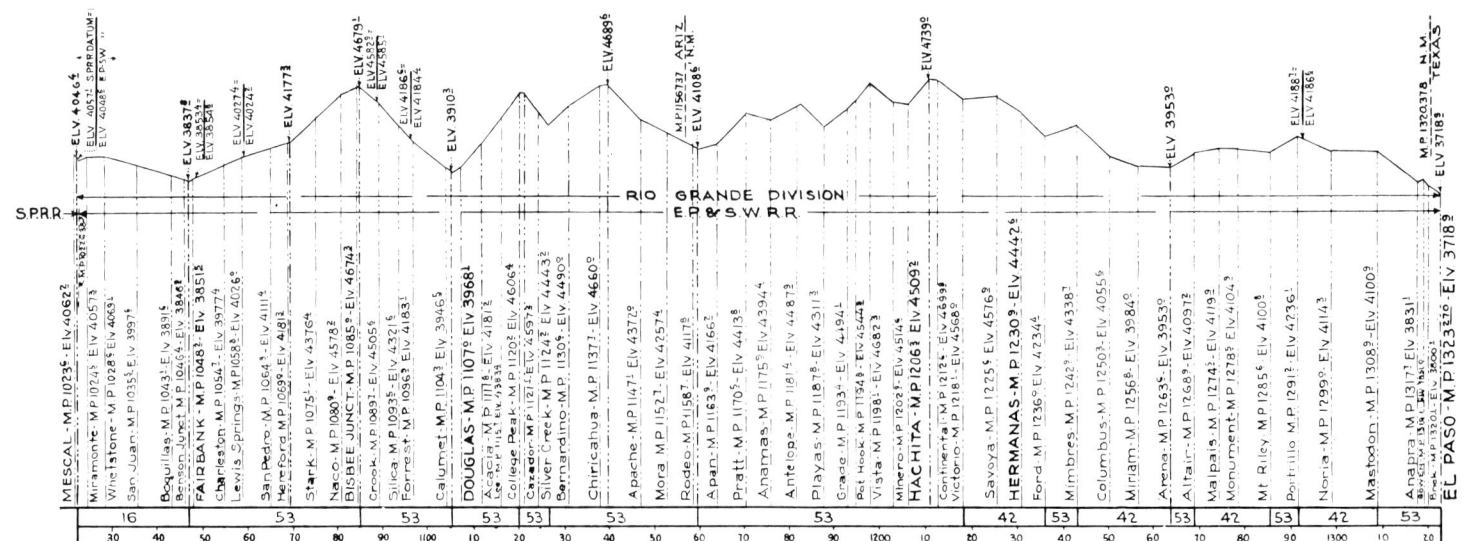

MESCAL TO EL PASO
VIA DOUGLAS

The eastbound *Golden State Limited* charges up a slight grade leaving Tucumcari, N.M., with 13 cars at 40 mph. The date is May 11, 1940, and this is Mt-2 territory. R.H. Kindig photo, A. Menke collection.

Sunset – Golden State Route

FROM THEIR inaugural run on January 6, 1924, until steam on this route was eventually displaced in the early 1950s, the 4300s played a major role in passenger and freight operations on both the Sunset and the connecting Golden State Routes. They eventually replaced 4-6-2 Pacifics on all the name trains and as their ranks grew it was not uncommon to see them double-headed when helpers were needed on long, heavy passenger trains. The Golden State Route's prime train was the *Golden State Limited*, Nos. 3-4. It operated between Los Angeles and Chicago, running on the old EP&SW route via Douglas between Tucson and El Paso and

then on to connect with the Rock Island at Tucumcari.

Other trains operating via Tucumcari to Chicago were the *Apache*, Nos. 11-12, which ran until February 13, 1938; the *Californian*, Nos. 13-14 until January 3, 1937, then Nos. 43-44 until May 18, 1947. The Mt-2's were standard passenger power east of El Paso to Tucumcari on all these trains. Helpers were seldom needed eastbound or westbound over this portion of the line. After the Mt-2's were converted to oil, they roamed as far west as Tucson and from time to time reached Los Angeles in regular service. They were even seen at Mission Bay, San Francisco, in 1945 before their

Tucson was a crew change point and locomotive service stop for engines. This Westbound troop train is running as a 2nd section of No. 375. Trains 375-376 operated 9-12-43 to 6-1-46, Tucumcari to Tucson only. West of Tucson they operated as an extra or 2nd section of regular passenger trains.

eventual transfer to the Sacramento Division in 1948.

Flagship of the Sunset Route was its namesake, the *Sunset Limited*. The route was open as far as El Paso on May 19, 1881; to the Pecos River crossing by January 15, 1883; and on February 1, 1883, through trains began operating Los Angeles to New Orleans. The *Sunset Limited* and its early predecessors operated since that date under various numbers and schedulings, from weekly to daily runnings, becoming Nos. 1-2 on May 1, 1932. In addition, the *Argonaut*, Nos. 5-6, the *Imperial*, Nos. 39-40, the *Arizona Limited*, Nos. 29-30, and the *Cherokee*, Nos. 43-44, along with numerous fast mail and express trains, all traversed this route and required the services of the powerful 4-8-2's.

The major operating problem on the west end of this route was Los Angeles Division's Beaumont Grade between Colton and Indio. On a heavy eastbound passenger, often the point helper was run with the train right out of Los Angeles Union Terminal to Indio. Otherwise the helper would be added at Colton. Westbounds got a helper at Indio. Helper power was often another 4-8-2, but especially at Colton or Indio, 2-8-2's, 2-10-2's and even cab-forwards were used to assist over Beaumont. When the 4-8-4's took over some

of the name trains, the Mt's were most often the Beaumont helpers.

The arrival of the 4-8-4's released some of the 4300s for other duties. During World War II they were the mainstay of power that moved thousands of soldiers in what sometimes seemed to be an endless line of troop trains moving east and west. They were used on this route to move high priority express reefer trains, and assignment to fast freight service was common.

The 4300s did not operate east of El Paso on the SP's Texas and New Orleans lines and no Mt's were ever owned by T&NO. Passenger trains over this route were hauled in the 1920s by P-5, P-6, and P-9 class 4-6-2's. In 1928 T&NO took delivery of the SP's largest and heaviest 4-6-2's, three engines classified P-13, Nos. 631-633. They were very similar to the 4-8-2's in specifications and lines. With 45,850 lbs. of tractive effort they could easily high-wheel the varnish across the Texas and Louisiana topography. In 1930 the T&NO received four new GS-1 4-8-4's, and in 1941, six Pacific Lines GS-1's were transferred to T&NO. In 1943, one more GS-1 was transferred and these 11 engines, along with the big Pacifics, provided power for the Sunset Route's passenger trains from El Paso to New Orleans. ■

Note — On the Southern Pacific all trains heading towards San Francisco are classified "westbound", and all trains heading away from San Francisco are classified "eastbound". Thus a train headed north from L.A. to S.F. is "westbound". A train heading north from S.F. to Portland is "eastbound". "Northbound" and "southbound" are merely terminologies indicating geographic direction and are not railroad terms. Eastbounds had even train numbers, westbounds had odd numbers.

A high-priority mail and express, running as the second section of the *Sunset*, roars up a slight grade on its race to the west. The raised lettering on No. 4300's tank is evident.

Train No. 102, the *Sunset Limited* (the train changed numbers from 101-102 to 1-2 on May 1, 1932), pauses at Colton to take on water. Fresh 3-year old 4319 will also receive a point helper here. May 5, 1927. R.P. Middlebrook photo.

Above — Hot desert sun glares down on the "Sunset" as it pauses at Indio. Sept. 27, 1937. W. Whittaker.

Below — Trains 47-48 were "Mail" with a rider coach, operating between Tucumcari-Los Angeles. 4386 has change here, west of Tucson. September, 1947. Jim Ady photo.

Above — The New Orleans bound "Argonaut" eases out of Tucson. The AC helper will go through to Dragoon to keep the 20 car train "on the advertised". August 31, 1952. A. Phelps photo.

Below — Second section of manifest 824 East prepares to leave Los Angeles. The road engine 4-10-2 will get an assist from 4307 to Beaumont. August 7, 1938. A. Menke collection.

The "Lark" charges through Burbank Junction in early morning light as it races to complete its overnight run to Los Angeles. April, 1933. Jeff Winslow collection.

MAIN LINE
SAN FRANCISCO TO SANTA BARBARA
VIA COAST LINE

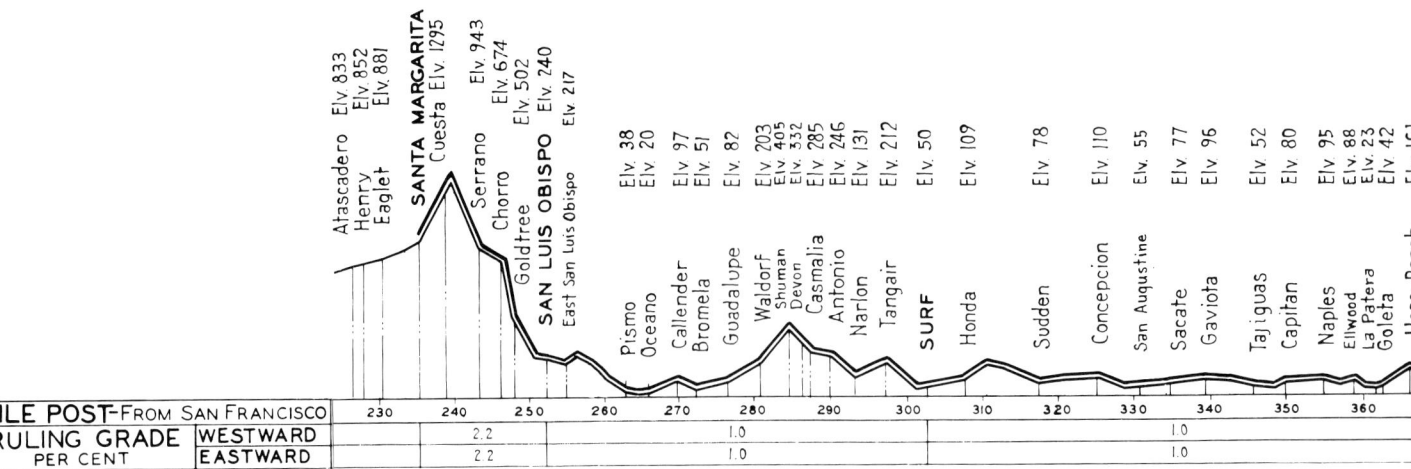

MILE POST-From San Francisco		230	240	250	260	270	280	290	300	310	320	330	340	350	360
RULING GRADE PER CENT	WESTWARD		2.2			1.0						1.0			
	EASTWARD		2.2			1.0						1.0			

4317 has an easy time working upgrade at Goldtree siding just out of San Luis Obispo. In a few minutes it will have rounded Horseshoe Curve and will be up at Chorro, where the line poles are evident at the top left of the photo. May 1, 1949. W. Whittaker photo.

Coast Route

THE SOUTHERN PACIFIC publicized its 471-mile Coast Route as the most beautiful train ride in the world. The line ran along the Pacific shore for 113 miles and the traveling public placed heavy demand on this route's trains, from the inception of through operations between San Francisco and Los Angeles. On December 6, 1901, the first scheduled through passenger train, the *Coast Line Limited*, Nos. 1-2 (Nos. 21-22 after Nov. 15, 1902), began service, and was advertised as a "daytime" or "daylight" train. In 1906 the *Shore Line Limited*, Nos. 19-20, was inaugurated. The first night passenger train on the line was the *Sea Shore Express*, Nos. 17-18, beginning service on Dec. 1, 1906. On May 8, 1910, the all-Pullman *Lark*, Nos. 75-76, began making the Los Angeles-San Francisco night run.

The *Daylight Limited* was born on April 28, 1922,

running as Nos. 71-72, on an operating stops-only basis. No passengers were taken en route between San Francisco and Los Angeles. Initially the road engines were the P-8 4-6-2's. The train's popularity, and public demands at some of the large intermediate communities, prompted the Espee to drop the limited status in 1928, and make several passenger stops along the route. By 1931, the train was longer and heavier and taxing the limits of the P-8 class locomotives to maintain the schedule. The big Mountain locomotives took over the assignments for the *Daylight*, and held that position until the train received lightweight equipment along with the streamlined GS-2 class 4-8-4's as motive power on March 21, 1937. 4300s were also in command of the *Lark* and another night train, the coach-tourist sleeper *Coaster*, Nos. 69-70, in the 1930s and 1940s.

The "Overnight" gallops up the Peninsula towards its San Francisco destination, bringing 12 cars, a rider coach and a caboose.

The only helper district on the Coast Route was over Cuesta grade between San Luis Obispo and Santa Margarita. The demanding 2.2% grade necessitated a helper engine, usually a 2-10-2, to assist a 4-8-2 on the grade. Point helpers were put on at San Luis Obispo for westbounds and Santa Margarita for eastbounds, and ran over Cuesta between these two points. When the "Daylight" 4-8-4's came, the 4300s were used to assist them on occasion, but the 2-10-2 remained the most common Cuesta helper for both passenger and freight trains. On many occasions, the all-purpose 4300s were even used here as rear helpers on freights.

Perhaps no other train the 4300s handled on this route captured the imagination as much as the "Overnights." Officially known on the timecard after World War II as the *Coast Merchandise*, Nos. 373-374, these fast freights provided overnight package service for Los Angeles and San Francisco-Oakland merchants. The men who operated them affectionately called them the "Ghosts," and ghosts they were. The long string of black boxcars streaking through the darkness at passenger speeds, the locomotive laying down a thin veil of steam over the car tops, justified the name. Made up of boxcars with high-speed trucks from a pool of 450 cars especially equipped for this service, the "Ghost" had its own paint scheme. The cars were painted entirely black with the usual SP medallion on a yellow background. An insignia of a red ball with a yellow arrow through it, and the word "Overnight" on the arrow, emphasized the service. These boxcars averaged 219 miles traveled each 24 hours, contrasting with a daily 16 miles average for other boxcars on railroads in the late 1940s.

The "Ghosts" were blocked in reverse from usual freights. Standard freight trains had the shortest-run cars next to the engine, the next shortest following, and so on. But the "Ghosts" started the run with the shortest haul next to the caboose, because the road engine was not cut off during the entire 471-mile run. All setouts and pickups were made from the rear of the train by waiting switcher crews. The same locomotive went all the way through, brought another "Overnight" back the next night, and repeated the performance the third and fourth nights. These hotshot trains operated Monday through Thursdays, four nights a week.

Mt-5 4374 works a freight extra across the San Francisquito Creek bridge at the edge of Palo Alto. October 4, 1941. W.C. Whittaker photo.

The massive 4300s were standard power for the "Overnights." Their sister 4400s joined them when the diesels began taking over passenger assignments. A 4300 could handle 22 boxcars and a caboose over Cuesta grade unassisted, and with that length a 4-8-2 would really have to knuckle down and show its grit to make the time over Cuesta. If the "Ghost" was longer than 22 cars, a point helper was added for the climb. The north and southbound trains usually met at Santa Margarita and the same helper was used on both trains. The remainder of the trip beyond the Cuesta really al-lowed the Mt's to stretch their legs in mile-a-minute plus running on "Ghosts" or other passenger and mail assignments.

The 4300s could be found, especially in later years, racing "reefer" hotshots from Salinas to connecting points at Roseville, or Santa Maria to Los Angeles, for eastbound produce. San Luis Obispo usually had one or two 4-8-2's assigned there as helpers while on standby as emergency passenger power. Of course, at San Francisco there were commuter assignments. These are discussed separately, p. 137. ∎

The "Coast Mail" drifts downgrade at Chorro, with the P-5 point helper assisting from Santa Margarita to San Luis Obispo. W.C. Whittaker photo.

Above — 4339 rushes the northbound "Coaster" through Watsonville Junction in this early 1930's scene. Note the well maintained roadbed. Jeff Winslow collection.
Below — Same locomotive in June, 1942, heads a long troop train extra near Glendale. Jim Ady photo.

Mt's were sometimes used out of San Luis Obispo as helpers. Here 4340 assists No. 99, the *Daylight*. November, 1951. Art Laidlaw photo.

Right – Engine 4305 glides down around Horseshoe Curve with No. 72 in May, 1949. By this time, the train normally had only a rider coach. The three Pullmans must have been a special movement. W.C. Whittaker.

Below – Mt-1 4311 heads train 72 at King City, with a typical consist of three 60-ft. baggage cars, an 80-ft. horse-baggage, an RPO, and two coaches, on July 13, 1947. W.C. Whittaker photo.

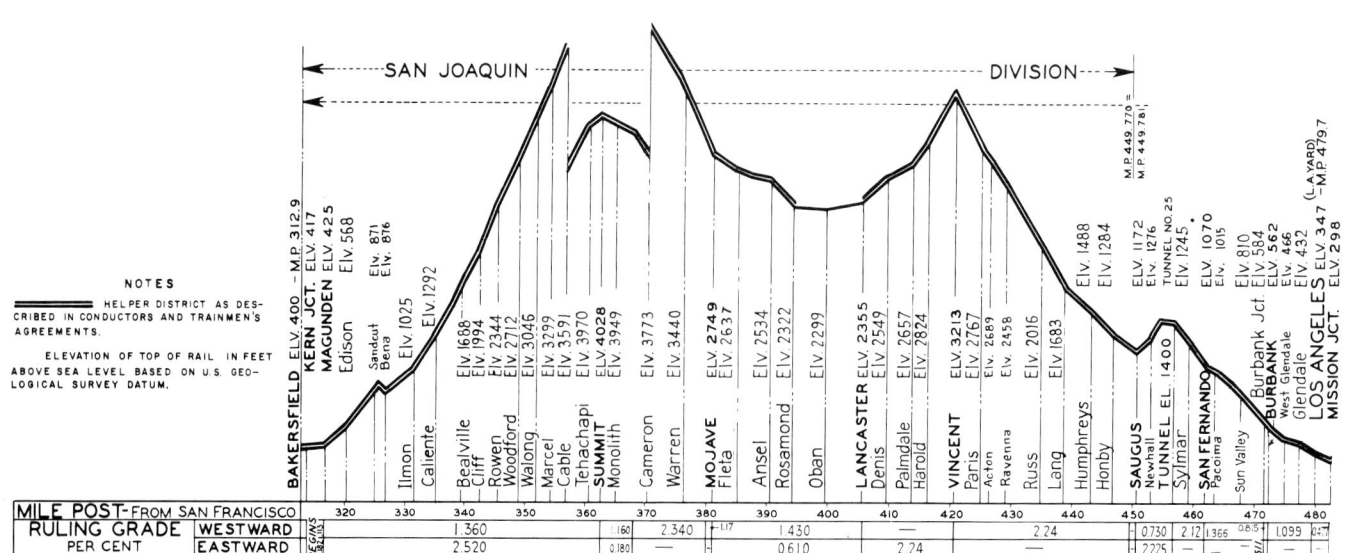

The Tehachapi Loop lies about 2 miles south of the summit, and this engineering feat allowed the railroad access to the summit with a compatible grade. Here, an eastbound freight starts out of the siding after waiting for a meet with "51", seen gliding downgrade and about to head into the tunnel to pass under the freight. The freight's mid-train helper is just to the left of the hill.

SAN JOAQUIN — DIVISION

NOTES

HELPER DISTRICT AS DES-CRIBED IN CONDUCTORS AND TRAINMEN'S AGREEMENTS.

ELEVATION OF TOP OF RAIL IN FEET ABOVE SEA LEVEL BASED ON U.S. GEO-LOGICAL SURVEY DATUM.

BAKERSFIELD ELV. 400 — M.P. 312.9
KERN JCT. ELV. 417
MAGUNDEN ELV. 425
Edison ELV. 568
Sandcut Elv. 871
Bena Elv. 876
Ilmon
Caliente Elv. 1025 Elv. 1292
Bealville Elv. 1688
Cliff Elv. 1994
Rowen Elv. 2344
Woodford Elv. 2712
Walong Elv. 3046
Marcel Elv. 3299
Cable Elv. 3591
Tehachapi Elv. 3970
SUMMIT ELV. 4028
Monolith Elv. 3949
Cameron Elv. 3773
Warren Elv. 3440
MOJAVE ELV. 2749
Fleta Elv. 2637
Ansel Elv. 2534
Rosamond Elv. 2322
Oban Elv. 2299
LANCASTER ELV. 2355
Denis Elv. 2549
Palmdale Elv. 2657
Harold Elv. 2824
VINCENT ELV. 3213
Paris Elv. 2767
Acton Elv. 2689
Ravenna Elv. 2458
Russ Elv. 2016
Lang Elv. 1683
Humphreys Elv. 1488
Honby Elv. 1284
SAUGUS Elv. 1172
Newhall Elv. 1276
TUNNEL NO. 25
TUNNEL EL. 1400
Sylmar Elv. 1245
SAN FERNANDO Elv. 1070
Pacoima Elv. 1015
Sun Valley Elv. 810
Burbank Jct. Elv. 584
BURBANK Elv. 562
West Glendale Elv. 466
Glendale Elv. 432
(L.A. YARD)
LOS ANGELES ELV. 347 — M.P. 4797
MISSION JCT. ELV. 298

M.P. 449.770
M.P. 449.781

MILE POST-FROM SAN FRANCISCO		320	330	340	350	360	370	380	390	400	410	420	430	440	450	460	470	480
RULING GRADE	WESTWARD		1.360				1.160	2.340	1.17	1.430	—		2.24		0.730	2.12 1.366 0.65	1.099 0.7
PER CENT	EASTWARD		2.520				0.180	—		0.610	2.24				2.225	—	6.11	

Train No. 51, the *San Joaquin Daylight*, has just stopped at Lathrop where the power for the *Sacramento Daylight* waits. Baggage will be transferred and coaches to Sacramento cut off. No. 51 will continue west to Oakland. The 4-4-2 will couple to the coaches, back around the south leg of the wye junction, and then head back to Sacramento. July, 1947. Guy Dunscomb photo.

San Joaquin Valley Route

EXCEPT FOR VARIATIONS in climate and geology, the Tehachapi Mountains that lay across the southern end of the great Central Valley presented obstacles similar to those the railroad encountered in the high Sierra. Access to Los Angeles required a 50-mile climb from Bakersfield over a 2.52% grade, and the line, to gain the crest of the grade at 4028 feet elevation, included one of railroading's engineering marvels, the famed Tehachapi Loop. Ever since the last spike was driven at Lang on September 5, 1876, the formidable mountain barrier has presented operating problems for the Southern Pacific. Consequently, because easier routing of Los Angeles-San Francisco passengers was gained via the Coast Line, the Valley Route did not see the services of as many name trains.

The Valley's original overnight train, which was the *Lark*'s counterpart, was the *Owl Limited* that began operating December 18, 1898, as Nos. 25-26, between Los Angeles and San Francisco on a 14 hour, 45 minute schedule. It became the *Owl* in July, 1920, and changed to Nos. 57-58 on June 2, 1946. The *West Coast* connected Los Angeles to Portland via Sacramento, operating as Nos. 59-60 in the Valley from 1924 until it was discontinued on December 7, 1960. It operated under different numbers north of Sacramento.

The Queen of the Valley Route was certainly the *San Joaquin Daylight*, Nos. 51-52, which began service as the *San Joaquin Flyer* effective March 20, 1927. On July 4, 1941, the train was streamlined with lightweight equipment except for head end and dining cars. At first the motive power for the newly equipped trains were three Class P-10 4-6-2's, engines 2484-2486, which were streamlined with skyline casing and "Daylight"-type skirting. They were painted in "Daylight" red and orange and were very striking, even with the flat smokebox front and cylindrical tender. The popularity of the new trains soon increased the length beyond the capabilities of the Pacifics, so the Mt's were called upon

The *West Coast* operated under Nos. 59-60, between Los Angeles and Sacramento. The train is seen here near French Camp with Mt-5 4374 in April, 1949. Guy Dunscomb photo.

to become the standard power. Five engines, 4350, 4352, 4353, 4361, and 4363, all Mt-4's, were assigned to Nos. 51-52, and all received special paint schemes. The cab sides and the tenders received the "Daylight" scheme. The engines had the skyline casing, but no Mt's were ever equipped with skirting. All five engines had 16,000-gallon Vanderbilt tenders at the time they had the special paint scheme.

The stiff 2.24 percent grade for northbounds between Saugus and Vincent through Soledad Canyon and the 2.34 percent rise from Mojave to Summit normally required two engines on any lengthy passenger train out of Los Angeles, all the way to Bakersfield. The Mt helper on No. 51 would cut off there, was serviced, and returned as point helper on No. 52 back to Los Angeles. It was a pretty sight to see the *San Joaquin Daylight* working over the Tehachapis with double-headed 4300s in "Daylight" colors.

Anything from 4-6-2's to 4-8-8-2's were occasionally used as point helpers, especially on the heavyweight trains. In the pre-lightweight era, it was not uncommon to see two AC's on the point of a long, heavy train. An Mt, or in later years a GS, would then take the train in the Valley. Valley Route trains entered Oakland by the line that cuts off at Tracy and runs along the Delta and Suisun Bay via Martinez. No passenger trains operated over Altamont Pass and Niles Canyon between Tracy and San Jose except the short *Fresno Flyer* which ran for a few years and used power smaller than 4-8-2's. But there were occasions, as in 1952, when severe rain caused washouts on the Coast Route, and the *Lark* and *Coast Daylight* detoured through the Valley.

When diesels began taking over assignments from GS 4-8-4's on other routes (the southwestern desert divisions were first to dieselize because of the bad water), they too were assigned to the Valley Route's trains. The *San Joaquin Daylight* was the last of SP's passenger trains to be dieselized. Steam hauled the trains the final time on September 14, 1956, before the Alco PAs took over. The 4300s were routinely used in the Valley on manifest freights and especially during the harvest season to rush long strings of "reefer" blocks filled with produce and fruit to Roseville where the cars were iced and sent on to northern and eastern markets. ∎

The inaugural run of the "Sacramento Daylight" with lightweight equipment rushes past Brighton Tower near Sacramento, behind 4363, on June 2, 1946.

For a short time there was a Modesto-Sacramento local, trains 261-262. It may have been the only train running solely between the two cities. It and "51" are seen here at Modesto. As soon as the big Mt rolls out, the 4-4-2 will be hot on its tail. March, 1944. Guy Dunscomb photo.

4345 and 2-8-2 3241 work a manifest over Altamont Pass. This was normally a freight only line. Jeff Winslow collection.

Extra 4320 crosses the Benicia Bridge over the Suisun Bay arm of the San Francisco Bay. Here the line from Roseville meets the line from Tracy. A. Menke collection.

Above — Snow slides in the Sierras have closed the Overland Route so here at Mojave we see the 28 car combined "21" (Mail) and "23" (Gold Coast) bellowing twin pillars of steam as it charges out of town to do battle with the Tehachapis. The train was routed Ogden-Barstow over the U.P. and over the Santa Fe to Mojave. January 19, 1952. Al Phelps photo.

Below — Valley Trains 55-56 were mail-coach, LA-Oakland, were discontinued Jan. 1, 1955. Shown here at Modesto. Guy Dunscomb photo.

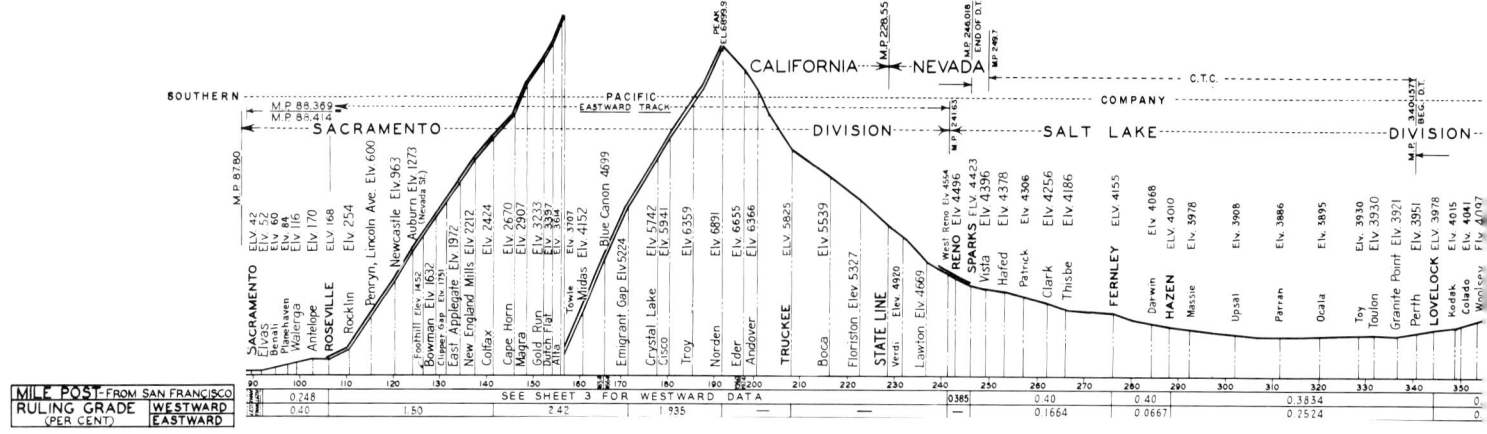

MILE POST–FROM SAN FRANCISCO		
RULING GRADE (PER CENT)	WESTWARD	
	EASTWARD	

MAIN LINE
SAN FRANCISCO TO OGDEN
VIA DAVIS AND ROSEVILLE
OVERLAND ROUTE
Part I–San Francisco to Rye Patch

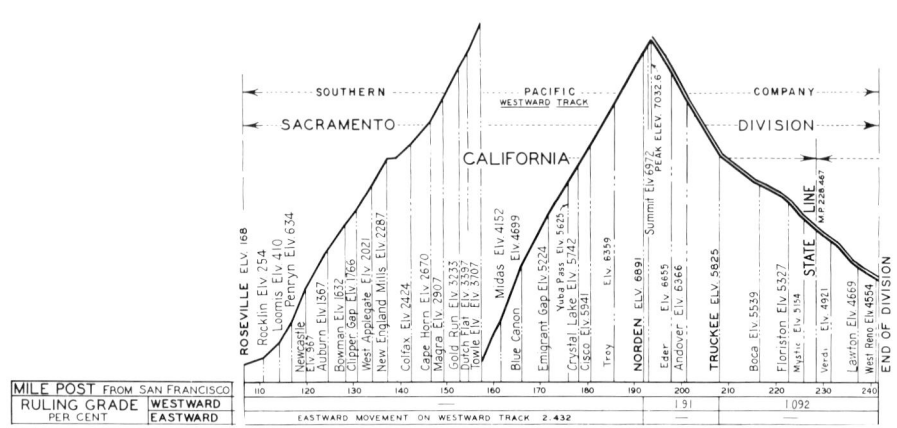

MILE POST FROM SAN FRANCISCO		
RULING GRADE PER CENT	WESTWARD	
	EASTWARD	

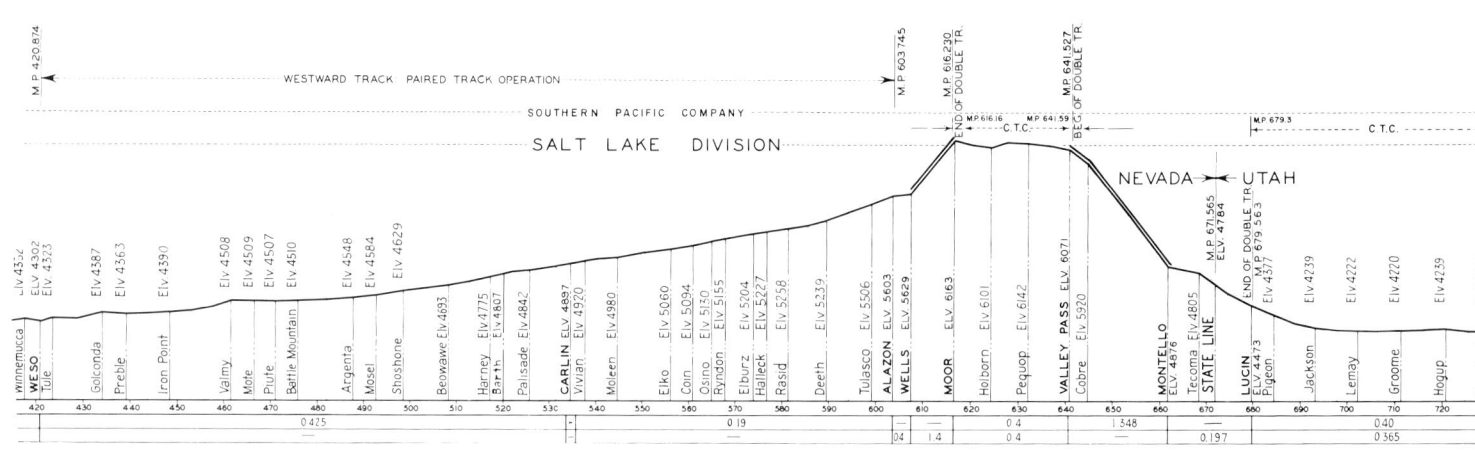

MILE POST–FROM SAN FRANCISCO		
RULING GRADE PER CENT	WESTWARD	
	EASTWARD	

The *Overland Limited* storms up the Sierra grade near Towle. June, 1947. W.C. Whittaker photo.

Overland Route

THE VAST DESERT expanse of Utah and Nevada provided ideal territory over which 4300s could run as they were intended to, on long, sustained, high-capacity trips where power and speed were both required. Daily passenger operations started on this first transcontinental route on May 15, 1869, five days after the driving of the golden spike at Promontory, Utah. Carded as Nos. 1-2, the train ran westward as the *Pacific Express*, and eastward as the *Atlantic Express*. The Sacramento-Chicago run took 5 days, 7 hours. On October 15, 1899, Nos. 1-2 became the renowned *Overland Limited*. By 1931 this schedule had been cut to 58 hours and was further reduced to 48 hours by 1947.

The 4-8-2's were the primary power used on this train and on all the Overland passenger trains after their arrival. When the GS-4 locomotives were delivered in 1941, they relieved many GS-3's of Coast Route duties. Eleven GS-3's were assigned to the Salt Lake Di-

vision, and these engines shared the calls with Mt's on passenger, fast mail and freight assignments until steam was withdrawn from service. Other 4-8-4 classes were never regularly assigned to the Sparks-Ogden run.

The *Advance Overland Limited* with sleeper and chair cars operated from April, 1935, until September, 1937, when the *Challenger*, Nos. 87-88, was established and the *Advance Overland* discontinued. In 1926, the *Gold Coast*, originally Nos. 27-28, began service and ran until June, 1931, when it was discontinued in Depression cutbacks. It was re-established on October 1, 1947, to replace the *Challenger*, which was withdrawn from service on that date. The *Gold Coast* operated as Nos. 23-24 until June 9, 1955. Nos. 19-20, the new *Pacific Limited*, started service June 2, 1918, and ran with sleepers and coaches until October 1, 1947, when it became an all-headend train called *The Mail*, Nos. 21-22. In the summers of 1939 and 1940, from mid-May to

The *Pacific Limited*, train No. 21, is stretched out 13 cars long. Here the Mt's could really stretch their legs, running across the open, sage-covered Nevada desert. The 4372's whistle blows a salute to photographer Al Phelps as she rushes by on this hot day in July, 1938.

mid-September, the SP, UP, and C&NW operated the *Treasure Island Special*, during the opening of an International Exposition on Treasure Island in San Francisco Bay. These trains had no numbers but operated as extra fare supplements to the *City of San Francisco* and the *Forty-Niner*. When heavyweight passenger trains were heavy, it became standard to use an AC over the Sierra. A 4300 would usually assist eastbound to Norden as point helper. This chore was customary for the Mt-2's after they arrived in 1948. Truckee helper for westbound passenger trains was most often a 2-8-0.

Express reefer trains with high priority perishables for eastern markets often ran 20-30 cars per train. Over "the Hill" these trains had an AC as road engine and normally an Mt as point helper to maintain speed. Often an Mt would handle the train east of Sparks to Ogden. Another standard operation that involved the Mt's was on drag freights over "the Hill" known as the "Modoc Empties." These were freight empties returning to Oregon, but were sent via Sparks and Alturas over the Modoc Line to relieve Shasta Route traffic. These trains normally had an AC as road power and a 4300 as rear helper between Roseville and Norden.

The only other helper district on this route was on the Salt Lake Division, between Wells and Moor eastbound and Montello to Valley Pass westbound where the line crested the Pequop Mountains. At Wells or Montello the Mt's would get an assist with a point helper if the tonnage of the passenger or freight train necessitated extra tractive effort.

West of Roseville to Oakland the 4-8-2's were just as much at home high-wheeling freight as they were the "varnish," and there was no hesitation by the roundhouse foreman at Roseville to send an Mt out on a long freight heading west or up the "Eastside Line" via Chico to Gerber to connect with the Shasta Division. ■

Mt-5 4372 wheels a block of express reefers past Hafed, Nevada, on a Sparks-Ogden run. April 7, 1951. Al Phelps photo.

Above — A "RV FB" (Roseville Fruitblock) works up the Sierra grade near Auburn in July, 1952. At this period "RV FB's" had between 90-100 cars, over 5000 tons. Standard power was a 4-8-2 as point helper, an AC as road engine, and two AC's at the rear, one 4 cars head of the caboose, one 4 cars ahead of the rear engine.
Below — 4316 and a 2-8-0 work a heavy empty drag near Ozol, CA., July, 1950. Both photos, W. Whittaker.

Express Reefer trains had 20 to 30 cars, and a 4-8-2 was used as point helper to maintain speed. A rider coach was used on the rear. Cascade Bridge. July, 1950.

Right — Manifest 2-496 leaving Roseville on the "Eastside Line" through Chico to Gerber. Engine 4389. July, 1948. Guy Dunscomb photo.

Below — Train 25, the westbound "Mail" near Sacramento, June, 1949. W. Whittaker.

Above — Engines used in freight service, Sparks-Ogden, used auxiliary water cars. 4300 awaits to race her train of perishables east as soon as the refrigerator cars are re-iced. Sparks, October, 1947. Al Phelps photo.

Below — AC's normally handled heavy passenger trains over "The Hill". 4221 uncouples and 4365 will take "27" to Oakland. March, 1948. Guy Dunscomb.

Above — Eastbound X4360 works hard past Nevada Dock on San Francisco Bay on April 1, 1951.
Below — Eastbound troop train running as 2-28 has a Baldwin road switcher at Wells, Nevada, for the climb to Moor in the Pequop Mtns. May, 1952. Both photos Al Phelps.

The Forty-Niner

The eastbound "49" is a blur of motion as it races past Stege, Ca., February 11, 1940. Guy Dunscomb photo.

THE *FORTY-NINER*, a new all-Pullman train of streamline design was added to the Overland Route on July 11, 1937, and was operated jointly by Southern Pacific, Union Pacific and the Chicago & Northwestern. The train's name matched its running time of 49 hours. It made five round trips per month, staggering its schedule with the streamlined *City of San Francisco* for departure and arrival every three days of deluxe, high-speed service between San Francisco and Chicago. It connected with the *Twentieth Century Limited* and *Broadway Limited* at Chicago.

The train consisted of eight cars, all being rebuilt heavyweight cars except the rear two cars which were actually a twin-unit articulated lightweight built for the train. The exterior was painted a shade of metallic gray, set off by black and gold striping above and below the windows. From the front, the cars were: baggage-dormitory-kitchen car "Donner Lake," dining car "Angels Camp," bedroom-drawing-room car "Joaquin Miller," Pullman sleepers "James Marshall," "Captain John Sutter" and "Gold Run," and the articulated unit, cars "Advance" and "Progress." "Advance" was a duplex car containing 16 bedrooms, 7 of which were on an upper level. The second car, "Progress," had a compartment and three double bedrooms, two *en suite*, with a buffet and observation lounge in the rear half of the car.

For the duration of its running, 4-8-2's were the standard *Forty-Niner* power. Normally the road engine made the entire 781-mile Oakland-Ogden run. If the Mt's were changed, it was at Sparks. Service points en route for the engine were Roseville, Sparks and Carlin. The train was serviced at West Oakland and Chicago where it was washed, brakes and air conditioning checked, and wheels changed if necessary, averaging two new wheels a trip.

A point helper, usually a 2-8-0, was put on at Colfax for eastbounds, and at Truckee for westbounds. On this train, Colfax helpers were normally cut off at Emigrant Gap, though they sometimes ran through to Norden. The Truckee helper was cut off at Norden. If freight work tied up these 2-8-0 helpers, an AC would replace the 4300 and run over the Sierra between Roseville and Sparks singlehanded. The train operated until July, 1941, the last eastbound leaving Oakland on July 23rd. On July 26, 1941, the second *City of San Francisco* went into operation, replacing the *Forty-Niner*. ■

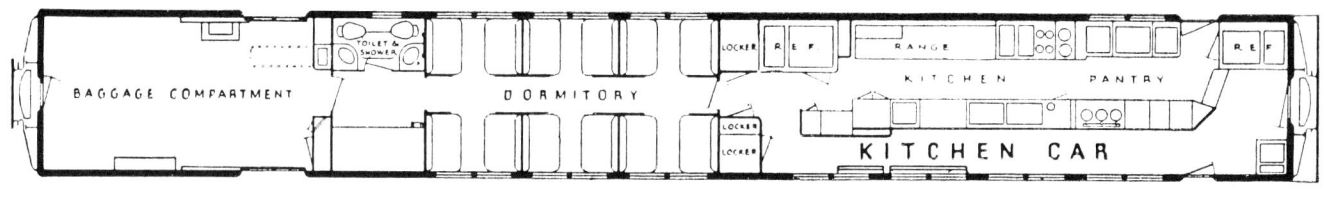

KITCHEN CAR

BAGGAGE COMPARTMENT   TOILET & SHOWER   DORMITORY   LOCKER   REF.   RANGE   KITCHEN   PANTRY   REF.

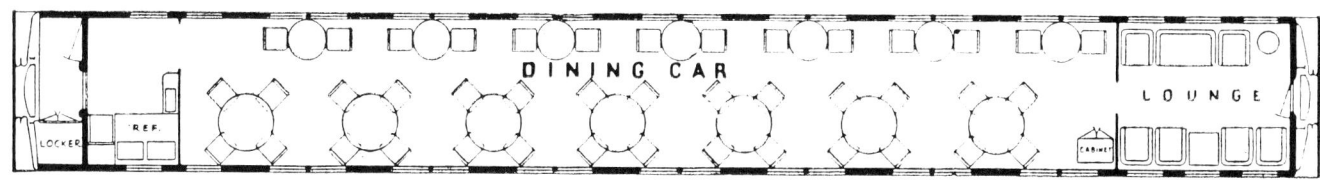

DINING CAR   LOUNGE

LOCKER   REF.   CABINET

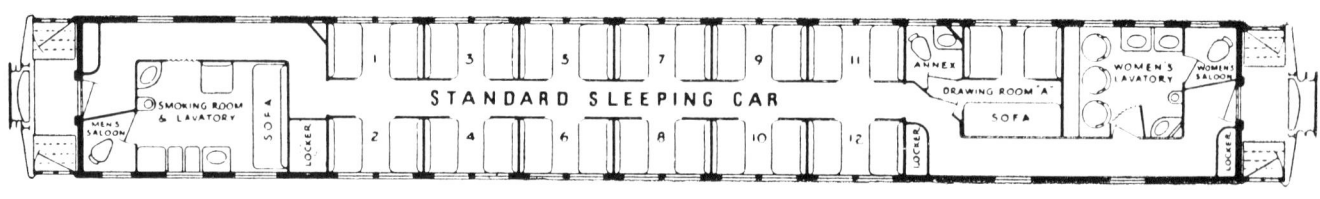

STANDARD SLEEPING CAR

MENS SALOON   SMOKING ROOM & LAVATORY   SOFA   LOCKER   ANNEX   DRAWING ROOM "A"   SOFA   WOMEN'S LAVATORY   WOMEN'S SALOON

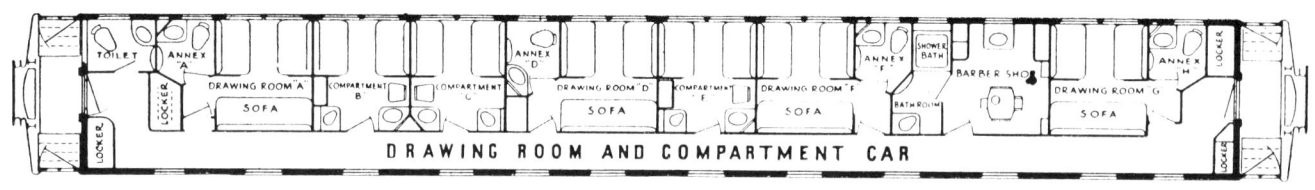

DRAWING ROOM AND COMPARTMENT CAR

TOILET   ANNEX "A"   LOCKER   DRAWING ROOM "A"   SOFA   COMPARTMENT "B"   COMPARTMENT "C"   ANNEX "D"   DRAWING ROOM "D"   SOFA   COMPARTMENT "F"   DRAWING ROOM "F"   SOFA   ANNEX "F"   SHOWER BATH   BATH ROOM   BARBER SHOP   DRAWING ROOM "G"   SOFA   ANNEX "H"   LOCKER

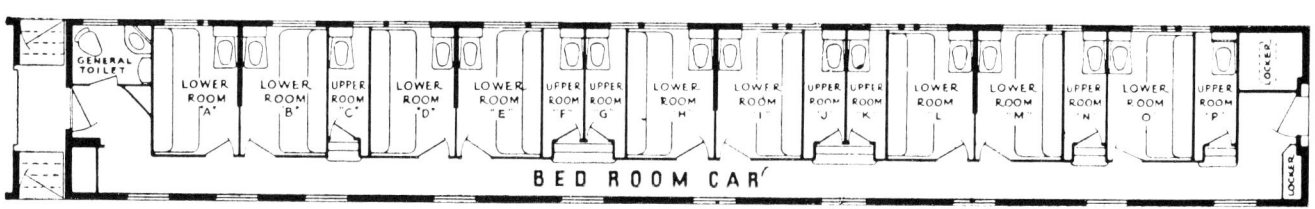

BED ROOM CAR

GENERAL TOILET   LOWER ROOM "A"   LOWER ROOM "B"   UPPER ROOM "C"   LOWER ROOM "D"   LOWER ROOM "E"   UPPER ROOM "F"   UPPER ROOM "G"   LOWER ROOM "H"   LOWER ROOM "I"   UPPER ROOM "J"   UPPER ROOM "K"   LOWER ROOM "L"   LOWER ROOM "M"   UPPER ROOM "N"   LOWER ROOM "O"   UPPER ROOM "P"   LOCKER

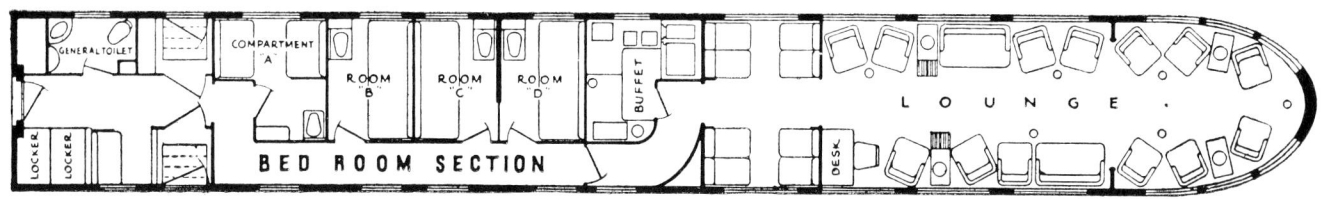

BED ROOM SECTION   LOUNGE

GENERAL TOILET   LOCKER   COMPARTMENT A   ROOM B   ROOM C   ROOM D   BUFFET   DESK

EQUIPMENT OF THE FORTY NINER

Left — Inaugural run of "49'er". The 4-6-2 took train to Roseville. Cab-Forward 4163 took train over "The Hill" to Sparks. 4376 ran Sparks to Ogden. Standard practice soon had one Mt running entire distance. July 11, 1937. Guy Dunscomb.

t — Engines assigned to the er" received extra white trim. Dunscomb photo.

ow — 4376 awaits in the evening at Sparks to rush the first east-nd "49'er" onto Ogden.

SPLIT SECOND SERVICE JOB

2:31½ PM - ARRIVAL of 49'er at Roseville. Foreman "mounts to the cabin" for inspection as incoming crew leave for roundhouse.

2:32 PM - WATER is given by the supplyman as the conductor keeps one eye on the watering operation and one eye on his watch.

2:33 PM - OIL is poured into right trailer journal box by machinist, who also checks many other spots in the course of this rapid-fire service job.

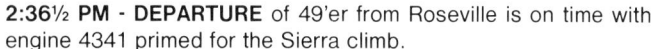

2:34 PM - GREASE is put into left main pin by machinist helper with air grease gun while the machinist inspects left No. 4 crank pin (and other parts) for loose nuts.

2:36½ PM - DEPARTURE of 49'er from Roseville is on time with engine 4341 primed for the Sierra climb.

2:35½ PM - WAITING engineer watches for the "highball" from the conductor, who signals as the service crew finishes. No passengers taken on at Roseville. Train stopped short distance from depot.

ON HER WAY - to the Sierra Summit, the 49'er charges through East Applegate.

First trip of 49'er" heads east out of Sparks as the evening sun glows low on the flanks of the sparkling train. On this run, to insure complete safety for the high speed passage of the train, all mainline switches were spiked prior to the train's arrival. July 11, 1937. Both photos Al Phelps.

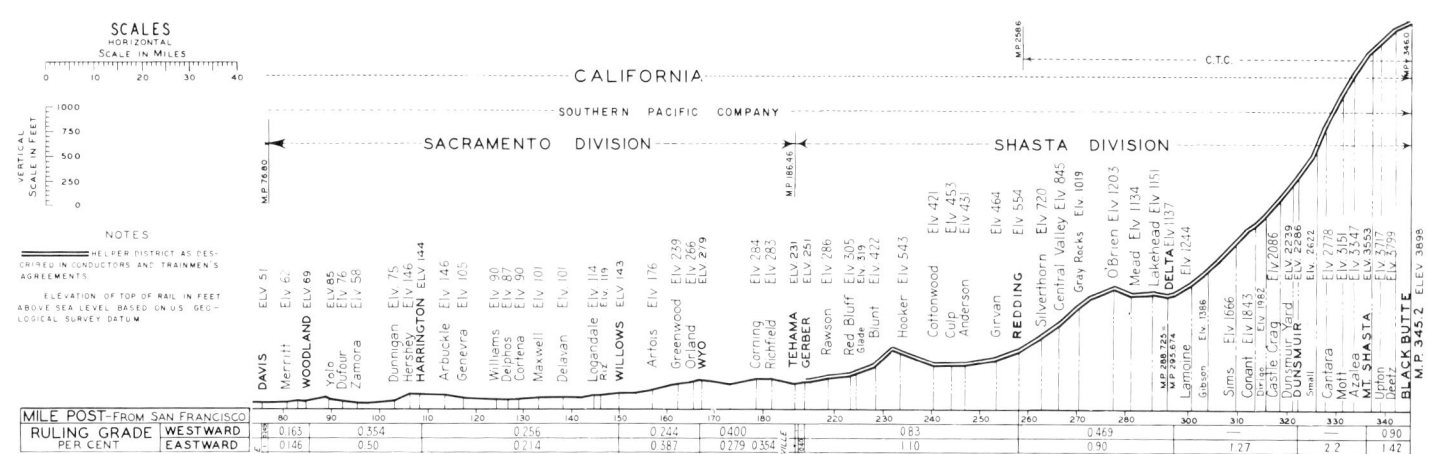

MAIN LINE
SAN FRANCISCO TO PORTLAND
PART I SAN FRANCISCO TO BLACK BUTTE
CASCADE ROUTE

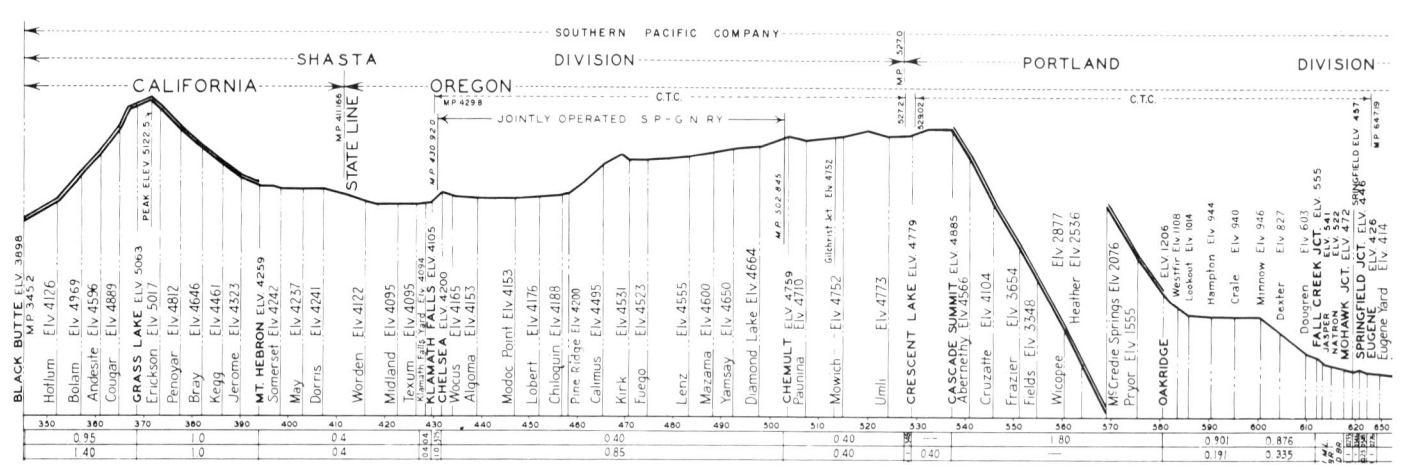

MAIN LINE
BLACK BUTTE TO SPRINGFIELD JCT.
VIA ASHLAND
SISKIYOU ROUTE

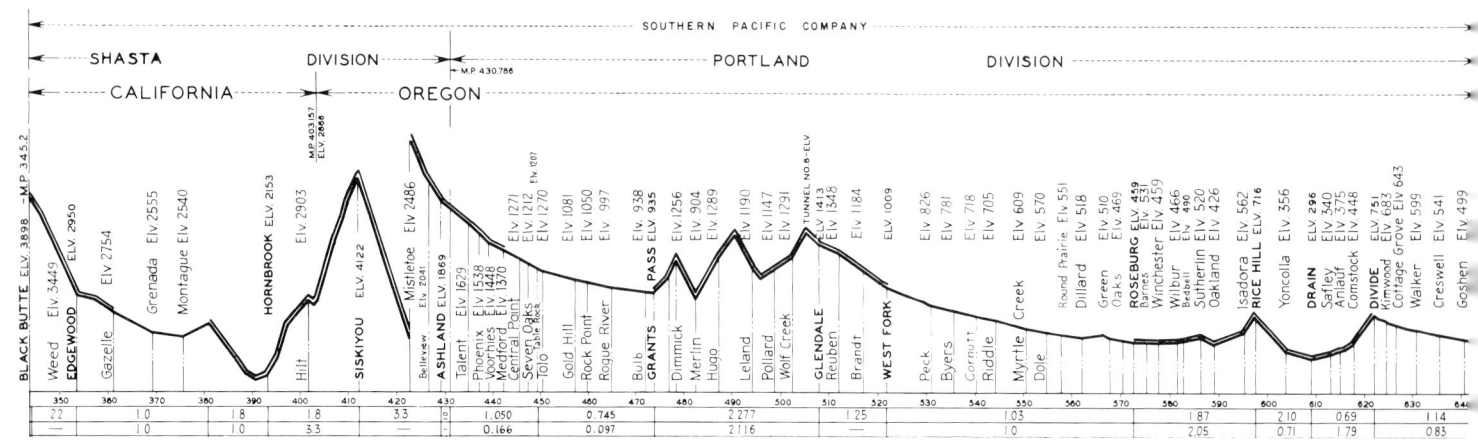

The *Shasta* near Shasta Springs, a few minutes out of Dunsmuir. August, 1949. Al Phelps photo.

Shasta Route

THE ORIGINAL ROUTE from Oakland to Portland was completed through the Siskiyou Mountains via Ashland, where the Oregon & California Railroad, building south from Portland, met the Central Pacific, the final spike being driven on December 17, 1887. The Natron Cutoff linking Klamath Falls to Eugene via a new line over the Cascade Mountains was opened on April 17, 1927. This line reduced the ruling grade from 3.3% over Siskiyou Summit to 1.8% on the westward ascent from Oakridge to Cascade Summit. The maximum grade for the entire new route was 2.2%, located on the original line, Dunsmuir–Black Butte.

The *Shasta Limited* came into being as Nos. 15-16 on October 21, 1895, on which date the former *Oregon & California Express* was renamed. This train operated over the Siskiyou Line with through sleepers to Seattle. It became Nos. 11-12 in October, 1899, and operated as such until May 1, 1931, when it was renumbered to Nos. 7-8. On Dec. 11, 1932, it became the *Shasta* between Eugene and Dunsmuir, connecting with the *Klamath* at Dunsmuir and the *Cascade* at Eugene. The 4300s were used for this train. The GS-1's and later GS classes were never rated over the line because of clearance restrictions. The longer 4400s could not operate in some curved tunnels; the booster engine piping would swing too wide and hit the timbers.

When the all-streamlined *Shasta Daylight* went into service on July 10, 1949, the *Shasta* exchanged its name for No. 328, Dunsmuir to Grants Pass, and No. 327, Grants Pass to Dunsmuir, connecting at Dunsmuir

Two sections of the *Oregonian* are being serviced at Klamath Falls. Crews changed here also. This train operated as Nos. 17-18 from June, 1937, to November, 1946. Jeff Winslow collection.

with the *Klamath*. These two trains were regularly hauled by 4-8-2's, Mt-1's 4319 and 4321 being assigned to the Shasta Division at Dunsmuir in the late 1940s specifically for these trains. An Mt could handle seven heavyweight cars Dunsmuir to Ashland without a helper. These trains operated until August 7, 1955, and were the last passenger trains to operate over the old Siskiyou Line.

Another train that operated over the Siskiyou Line was the *Oregonian*, which began San Francisco-Portland service in 1918 and ran as Nos. 53-54 until April 17, 1927, when it changed to Nos. 13-14 and operated as such, still over the Siskiyous, until May 1, 1931. Due to the Depression, service was then cut back Portland-to-Ashland only, and it was renumbered as Nos. 33-34. On Dec. 11, 1932, it became Nos. 329-330, operating between Eugene and Ashland and connecting at Eugene with the *West Coast*. Effective May 1, 1936, the two trains began running Portland-Ashland. On June 13, 1937, the *Oregonian* was reinstated as a through San Francisco-Portland train, renumbered as 17-18, and took over the *Cascade*'s equipment and schedules, as the *Cascade* went on a faster schedule with new heavyweight equipment. The *Oregonian* operated on this schedule over the Cascade Line until it was discontinued Nov. 14, 1946.

The *Rogue River*, Nos. 329-330, was renamed when the *Oregonian* was reinstated in 1937. It operated be-

tween Portland and Ashland with the 4-8-2's as standard road power. These trains also handled merchandise box cars, and were actually the last mainline mixed trains on the Espee. Southbound out of Portland it had around 20 cars, making drops at Eugene and Roseburg. Arriving in Ashland, it would usually have 3 merchandise cars, 1 RPO, 1 baggage, 1 chair car, 1 all-day lunch car, and a Pullman sleeper. Northbound, a 2-8-0 helper was used from Grants Pass to Glendale, just south of Roseburg, and pickups made at Roseburg and Eugene. The trains connected with Nos. 327-328 at Ashland.

The remaining trains on the Shasta Route were operated over the Cascade Line. On the same date that the line opened, a new train, the *Cascade*, Nos. 17-18, started operations. The *Cascade* became Nos. 19-20 effective Oct. 1, 1934, but returned to Nos. 17-18 on May 1, 1935. In June, 1937, it was re-equipped with new Pullman cars and operated until August 4, 1946, as Nos. 23-24. On that date it again received new heavyweight equipment and became Nos. 11-12. On August 13, 1950, it became all streamlined and diesel powered. The Mt's were standard power on this train until the GS-1's came in 1930. The GS-1's were designed specifically to make the entire San Francisco-Portland run.

Effective May 1, 1929, a new train, the *Klamath*, Nos. 7-8, began service between San Francisco and Portland, thus making five trains daily carrying Pullmans on the run between the two cities. Nos. 7-8 car-

A "California-Nevada Railroad Days" special makes a photo run-by near Castle Crags with Mt-5 4367. June 21, 1953. W.C. Whittaker photo.

ried standard and tourist sleepers and coaches and ran via Klamath Falls. On Dec. 11, 1932, the *Klamath* became Nos. 5-6, and operated via the Cascade Line between Dunsmuir and Eugene only. It connected at those two points with the *Shasta*, which was now running San Francisco-Portland as Nos. 7-8 via the Siskiyou Line. On April 1, 1933, northbound No. 6 was cancelled and only No. 5 operated between Eugene and Dunsmuir, with *Shasta* connections. The *Klamath* resumed separate operation, San Francisco-Portland, as Nos. 5-6 on April 1, 1935, becoming Nos. 19-20 effective May 1, 1936. This train carried many head-end cars and often was so heavy that two 4-8-2's were used right out of Portland to maintain speed. On Sept. 30, 1956, Nos. 19-20 became head-end trains only; the name *Klamath* was dropped.

The *Beaver* was another train with a 4-8-2 on the head end as standard power. Starting as a summer extra with no numbers on June 8, 1940, it was an economy train with tourist sleepers and coaches. Its popularity established it as an all-year train, Nos. 11-12, by September, 1940. Consolidated with the *Cascade* during World War II, it was re-established on August 4, 1946, as a separate train numbered 13-14, as the *Cascade* became 11-12. It was discontinued July 10, 1949, the date the streamlined *Shasta Daylight* went into service.

The *West Coast* was a Los Angeles-Portland train running via the Valley Route through Sacramento. Ser-

vice started Nov. 1,1924, as Nos. 14-15, carrying the name *Puget Sound Express* northbound and the *Southern California Express* southbound. The name *West Coast* and Nos. 15-16 were effective June 1, 1927. The train between Sacramento and Portland was discontinued on Oct. 2, 1949, but continued to operate as Nos. 59-60, Sacramento-Los Angeles, until Dec. 7, 1960.

Northbound trains climbing out of the Sacramento River Canyon to the shoulders of Mt. Shasta on the 2.2% grade between Dunsmuir and Black Butte required helpers. Until the early 1930s, all trains changed motive power at Dunsmuir, and 4300s were kept there for passenger assignments. A 2-10-2 was the usual helper power, but another 4-8-2 was not uncommon, and if these engines had other assignments, a 2-8-0 or even a 4-6-2 would lend the extra tractive power. These helper engines would go to either Black Butte or Grass Lake, depending on how heavy the train was. In the early 1930s, passenger power began running Oakland-Portland. Southbound trains definitely required a helper from Oakridge to Cascade Summit. If the train was long and heavy, a helper was sometimes put on at Eugene, and on occasion would even run all the way out of Portland, another 4-8-2 being most common as the point helper.

The 4-8-2's were rarely used between Gerber and Eugene in any kind of freight service, either as road engines or helpers. Train registers in Al Phelps' collection do show an instance in December, 1935, when No. 4339 ran as the Dunsmuir point helper with road en-

Train No. 15, which operated between Dunsmuir and Gerber, is shown here in the hole at Girvan for a freight. Dec. 7, 1940. Al Phelps photo.

Left – Train Nos. 329-330, the *Rogue River*, ran between Portland and Ashland, and was the last SP mainline mixed train, always carrying merchandise boxcars. Grants Pass, May 9, 1948. Al Phelps photo.

Right – Steam-powered No. 10 was a mail and express train that ran from Dec. 15 to Christmas for a few years. The streamlined *Shasta Daylight* was normally No. 10, so the mail train operated during these few days as a section of "10," same schedule. Dec. 19, 1953. Alan Aske photo.

gine 4348 on the *West Coast*, No. 16. The 4339 worked from Dunsmuir through Black Butte to Mt. Hebron, where it was cut off and turned on the wye. It then helped train 1-635, with road engine 3677, a 2-10-2, and a 2798-ton train, from Mt. Hebron to Grass Lake, cut off, and ran light down to Dunsmuir. It was an unusual move, but may have occurred more than once.

Most often 4-8-2 Dunsmuir helpers on passenger trains were cut off at Black Butte or Grass Lake, but in the late thirties and during World War II when the trains were 15 to 20 cars and heavy, it was fairly common for a 4300 to help the road 4300 or 4400 all the way from Dunsmuir to Klamath Falls. This was to maintain speed and keep the train on schedule. Train registers also show it was common practice during this period to double-head a 4300 with the road Mt or GS from Gerber to Oakland Pier or Sacramento, again to maintain schedule running time. Some trains such as the *Cascade* and *Beaver* were consolidated during this period, so long, heavy consists were the norm. It was quite a sight to see double-headed 4300s highballing a long string of varnish down the Sacramento Valley, or down from the shoulders of Mt. Shasta and across the Klamath Basin.

From Klamath Falls, the SP had a line that ran southeast along the eastern side of the Sierra to connect

Above – A busy train time at Klamath Falls. Two sections of the northbound *Klamath* are being serviced. The second section is actually a troop train and some Navy personnel are stretching their legs. At left is Great Northern locomotive 2012, a 2-8-8-0. It will pull out to run over the jointly operated GN-SP line from Klamath Falls to Chemult, Ore., after the sections of the *Klamath* leave. June, 1951. Al Phelps photo.

Right – Locomotive 4351 passes Pinole as it races the westbound *Klamath* toward Oakland Pier. March 3, 1946. W.C. Whittaker photo.

via Alturas with the Overland Route at Fernley, Nevada. Known as the Modoc Line, this route was completed on July 13, 1929, and allowed Pacific Northwest freight destined for Ogden connections to bypass Roseville and the steep Sierra crossing. The line also cut 210 miles off the total mileage via Roseville. Passenger service on this line in the 1920s was provided by *The Tahoe*, Nos. 31-32 (21-22 in later years), that connected with the *West Coast* at Klamath Falls and the *Pacific Limited* to Chicago at Fernley. The usual train was 4-5 cars, with through Pullman and dining car service provided until 1932. Motive power was normally a 4-6-0. The train became a tri-weekly Reno-Alturas coach run in 1932 and was discontinued in December, 1937.

At the Alturas engine house, steam aficionados could only find big freight maulers, AC-class 4-8-8-2's, with a couple of 2-8-0's that handled switching and worked the Lakeview branch, but no Mt-class engines. In 1953, the conventional cab-rear AC-9 2-8-8-4's came on the scene to run out their final miles. The only instances when a 4300 would venture across this line were when severe storms or landslides closed the Shasta Route. During the record winters of 1936 and again in 1940, when snowfall literally choked the Sacramento River Canyon above Dunsmuir and around Mt. Shasta, the *Klamath*, *Cascade*, and *West Coast* were all detoured via Alturas, the road Mt's going all the way through to Sparks. An occasional director's special provided the only other rare glimpse of an Mt on this isolated, high-country line. ■

Double heading usually meant balancing power since one engine could handle the normal trains. It certainly made a beautiful sight though. Engines 4303 and 2482. November 8, 1947. W. Whittaker photo.

Peninsula Commute
Steam's Finale

Evening lineup at Third and Townsend

THE CHANGEOVER FROM steam to diesel on the primary passenger trains was almost complete by the mid-1950s. The 4-8-2's had given way to 4400s on the primary name trains even earlier, so by 1950 the 4300s arrived in force to become the workhorses of the San Francisco Peninsula commuter fleet. The service they provided was the transporting of over 16,000 commuters each day between San Jose and San Francisco. The 47-mile double-track line was literally a race track during the hour or so before and after each work day.

Locomotives in this service presented a fine opportunity for the observer to see the big passenger engines working under the most demanding of situations. Trains were run as closely as three-minute intervals. There were no limiteds or expresses so no train ran around its predecessor. Some trains were 10 to 15 cars long, requiring extreme power from the locomotive and expert control by the crew. The stations being only a mile or two apart demanded the best acceleration and deceleration every few minutes. No sooner would the train gain momentum then it would start braking for the next stop.

The roundhouses at Mission Bay (San Francisco) and San Jose carefully maintained this fleet to keep it in top condition. Locomotives from each Mt class, with the exception of the Mt-2's, saw duty in commuter service. Most of the 4300s still had their boosters when assigned, and these were used for the fast getaways required at station stops.

Though the Mt's and GS's had run many miles by this time, they served admirably and dependably in the commute duty. By late 1956, time was running out, though, for all steam operations. Electro-Motive diesel F, GP, and SD units were taking over all freight movements, and the commute operations were to be the final stand for steam. The SP had purchased 16 Fairbanks-Morse Train Masters to operate in Arizona and New Mexico. The dusty desert runs were proving too destructive to the diesel prime movers, so the San Francisco Main Office decided to bring them west for commute service. They arrived in January, 1957, and struck the death knell for the remaining steam power. In a matter of a few days the calls for the steamers dwindled to just a handful. No one could anticipate the

Above — Commute motive power was serviced at the Mission Bay roundhouse between runs. The 4376 eases off the turntable to back down to the Third and Townsend Station, afresh in new paint after receiving what would be her final shopping. Jim Orem photo: 1956.

Below — Train 132 ran southbound, San Francisco to Menlo Park, then over the Los Gatos branch. Because there was no wye, the engine ran around the train and pulled the train backwards to San Jose. No. 2476, a 4-6-2, usually handled this job and its tender was equipped with a backup pilot. The service ended January 27, 1964. Shown here at Del Monte. W. Whittaker photo.

Above — The new double deck commute cars arrived in June, 1955, and they were on hand when steam was king. Summer, 1956, at San Bruno. W. Whittaker photo.
Below — 4342 wheels a San Francisco bound commuter past Burlingame. August 6, 1956. Al Phelps photo.

Sou Pac Co - Pac Lines
(Name of Railroad)

C.S.-2530

STATION RECORD OF TRAIN MOVEMENTS
EMPLOYEES ON DUTY

NAME	OCCUPATION	WENT ON DUTY	WENT OFF DUTY	WENT ON DUTY	WENT OFF DUTY
	Operator ✓	12 MID	8a		
	✓	8a	4 PM		
	✓	4 PM	12 MID		

Place _Roseville Calif.,_ Date _October 1st_ 19_50_

SYMBOLS FOR FREIGHTS

	EAST BOUND				WEST BOUND		
TRAIN	ENGINE	ARRIVED	TRAIN DEPARTED	TRAIN	ENGINE	TRAIN ARRIVED	DEPARTED
22	4338	103 AM	"MAIL"	X	4316	CAB-HOP	140 AM
26	4310	140 AM	LOCAL PASS.	23	4338	GOLD COAST	340 AM
X	2816	450 AM	SWING	21	6019-5918-6019	"MAIL"	440 AM
X	4389	610 AM	CAB HOP	X	4320	BROOM	447 AM
X	4357	650 AM	CAB HOP	25	4310	LOCAL PASS.	450 AM
X	4329	815 AM	DRAG	X	3615	LSP-29	510 AM
X	4315	955 AM	OVE-30	101	6014-5914-6013	"CITY OF SF"	623 AM
202	2467	1044 AM	GERBER PASS.	X	4319	CAB HOP	735 AM
X	4332	100 PM	SJVB-631	X	3308	✓ ✓	805 AM
X	3245	110 PM	SWING	X	4386	✓ ✓	810 AM
28	6020-5918-6019	209 PM	S.F. OVERLAND	X	2816	SWING	830 AM
X	4334	250 PM	SJVB-632	X	4389	CAB HOP	915 AM
X	4332	330 PM	SJVB-633	X	4361	APM-29	1055 AM
X	4310	530 PM	XAP	X	4344	CAB-HOP	200 PM
X	3308	550 PM	SUISUN TURN	X	4329	CS-29	240 PM
X	4360	710 PM	CAB-HOP	X	4315	STOCK SPECIAL	250 PM
X	4323	715 PM	WEST SIDE	X	3245	BROOM	300 PM
102	6014-5914-6013	749 PM	CITY OF SF	27	4465	S.F. OVERLAND	335 PM
24	4338	947 PM	GOLD COAST	X	4332	SALINAS REEFERS	445 PM
X	2361	1030 PM	LITE ENGINE	201	2361	LOCAL PASS.	653 PM
				X	6265-8165-8166	WEST SIDE	950 PM
				X	4322	1st CS-30	1130 PM
				X	4334	OVW-30	1140 PM

Symbol	Description
Swing —	Local frt. between Sacto. & Roseville, several times each day
Cab-Hop —	Engine & caboose only, picked up train at Sacto. or Davis.
O.V.E. —	Overland East. Frt. not passenger.
O.V.W. —	Overland West.
S.J.V.B. —	San Jose Vegetable Block.
X.A.P. —	Empty Auto Parts cars
Broom —	Local between Oakland to Roseville or vice versa. Picks up all loads and empties enroute, makes clean sweep!
Suisun Turn —	Roseville to Suisun-Fairfield and return.
West Side —	to or from Gerber via West side line, Davis and Willows.
L.S.P. —	Live Stock and Perishables.
A.P.M. —	Auto Parts Merchandise.
C.S. —	California special
Salinas Reefers —	Empty reefers for Salinas Valley, via Oakland, San Jose, Watsonville Jct.
X —	Extra train.

INSTRUCTIONS

1. This record shall be made at each station, tower, office or place from which the time of arrival, departure or passing of trains is reported by telegraph or telephone.
2. Each operator, signalman and leverman shall enter the time he goes on or off duty in the space provided for that purpose.

Note: Where number shows after symbols signifies origin date. Example CS-29 equals date from Ogden. Number such as S.J.V.B. - 631 indicates that this is the 631st vegetable block moved since the first of the year.

This operations sheet shows trains in and out of Roseville to and from Sacramento and Oakland. It does not cover trains from Tracy or Fresno, nor does it cover trains on "The Hill" or up the Valley. This shows the last great stand of the 4300's. Note some diesels are appearing. Mt's were used on both freight and passenger on this date. The Mt's handled 13 trains into Roseville and 14 trains out. Some engines show more than once. Example of this: Engine 4338 into Roseville on #22 at 1:03 A.M., immediately serviced and turned to go back on #23 at 3:40 A.M. It arrived Oakland at 8 A.M., laid over until 6 PM to return #24 at 9:47 P.M. Another example: Engine 4310 into Roseville on #26 at 1:40 A.M., turned, out on #25 at 4:50 A.M., arrived Oakland 10:00 A.M., returned Roseville on train XAP at 5:30 P.M. A remarkable record considering the miles these engines already had.

Train 494 winds through the crossovers and around the wye in front of the Roseville depot to head up the Eastside line, via Chico with a reefer block to Gerber. June 26, 1949. W. Whittaker photo.

last day would come so fast. On January 22, 1957, steam hauled commute trains for the final time. No more would the Mission Bay and San Jose roundhouses reverberate with the noise of atomizers and blowers as fires were ignited and life awakened in the resting steam giants. The fireboxes were cooled forever.

For nearly two decades, in the twenties and thirties, the Mt class 4300s dominated the system as "the" power for the Southern Pacific's fleet of name trains, mail and express, and high-speed freights. There was not a route over which they did not tread. No matter what the duty they proved, as railroad men testified, to be the most dependable and capable steam engine on the entire roster. When they were gradually displaced by the 4400s, they became the backbone of the system's fast freight service, hauling manifests and extra sections over the territories where the grades didn't require the tractive effort of the big cab-forwards.

It is ironic that the engines ended their active life near their birthplace. By the early 1950s, steam was gone from the desert divisions and high mountain districts. The central California divisions within an easy run of Sacramento were where the 4300s ran out their final miles. When the last call to service was completed, a historic era on the Southern Pacific came to an end. No more would the sounds and sights of big steam in action hasten the hearts of those who ran, maintained or just plain watched them. But for those who were affected by those magnificent steam locomotives, the memories will linger forever. ■

Bayshore roundhouse. Mt-5 4368 has tender No. 8796, class 160-C-1. P-8 4-6-2 No. 2468 has tender No. 8762, class 120-C-8. Dunscomb photo.

Tenders

4340 waits to help No. 99, the *Daylight*, at San Luis Obispo. The tender is 8919, Class 160-C-4. November, 1951. Art Laidlaw photo.

Data and Material Collected and Prepared
by
Arnold S. Menke

THE SOUTHERN PACIFIC used a wide variety of tenders during the steam era, from the typical small rectangular cars used in early years on all railroads, to some that were nearly unique to the Espee. Just as the massive cab-forward articulated locomotive was an SP trademark, so too were the "whaleback" tenders which resembled upside-down bathtubs. These were first introduced in 1901, and the railroad continued to refine them as late as 1950 in the form of rebuilds. The Vanderbilt tender, with its cylindrical water tank and box-like oil or coal compartment, was first used in

1902 and gained immediate favor with the Southern Pacific. The railroad eventually had a large fleet of these distinctive tenders which were used in various sizes with nearly all classes of locomotives, including the 4300s.

The advent of cast steel underframes with integral end sills ushered in the modern era of tender design. Among the first SP tenders so constructed were 12,000-gallon Vanderbilts built in 1921 for P-8's, F-3's and F-4's. Tenders of this type were also originally built for the Mt-1's in 1923. Eventually cast steel frames formed the bottom of the water tank itself, the so-called "water-bottom" frames. The 16,000-gallon Vanderbilt tenders constructed in 1927 for the Mt-4's and the SP-3's were the first of this type on the Southern Pacific. Except for some SP rebuilds, all tenders built from this time on were water-bottom design.

Most large railroads used classification systems for their tenders just as they did for their locomotives, and the SP was no exception. The Southern Pacific began their first tender classification system in 1913, and it was a simple one. Tenders were grouped only by their water capacity regardless of tank shape. Thus, for example, all 9,000-gallon tenders, whether rectangular or cylindrical (Vanderbilt) were in one class. Class symbols were based on an abbreviation of the water capacity. The symbol for a 9,000-gallon tender was 90. Each tender in the class was given a number preceded by the class symbol: 90-1, 90-2, 90-3, etc. This number was stenciled on the tender frame in white. Numbering of tenders under this system was rather haphazard, with no general adherence to original sequence of builder dates or locomotive sequences. Instead the tenders apparently were numbered in one class as they came into the shops for repair.

The second and final tender classification system was started early in 1922. Classes were separated according to tank shape as well as by water capacity. A letter (or letters) was added to the water capacity symbol to indicate physical appearance: C for cylindrical or Vanderbilt, R for rectangular, SR for sloping rectangular, and SC for semicylindrical or whaleback. Thus a 12,000-gallon Vanderbilt tender was indicated by the symbol 120-C. Since there was often more than one class of tenders of a given tank shape and water capacity each class was given a number: 120-C-1, 120-C-2, etc.,

to 120-C-8. Under the 1922 system each tender was given a four-digit number. This number, along with the tender class, was indicated on a 4 x 7-inch cast iron plate that was attached to the frame, one on each side. The first 1922 classification system number assignment appears to have been No. 8530 for a 120-C-1 tender built by Baldwin in July, 1922, for an F-4 class 2-10-2. Even under the 1922 system, numbers were often applied randomly to tenders built after the system was initiated. Locomotives of different classes often received tenders of the same class. In these cases tender numbers were rarely consecutive for one class of locomotive until 1937. Tenders built from 1937 on seem to have been consecutively numbered with respect to their associated locomotive numbers.

Tender numbers, like locomotive numbers, were "tied" to the frame. Even though tanks were modified and sometimes enlarged, the tender number usually remained the same. But rebuilds resulting in new classes often were given new numbers. The 123-R-1's of the Mt-2 class were rebuilt at El Paso to larger capacity 160-R-1's but they kept their original numbers. The SP rebuilt many tenders at its Sacramento, Los Angeles, El Paso, Bayshore and Ogden shops. The company also constructed quite a number of new tenders at the Sacramento and Los Angeles shops. The 160-C tenders used with the Mountains were among these.

Early fuel used by the Southern Pacific and the lines it took over was wood, coal or both. The railroad converted 4-4-0 No. 1344 to burn oil in May, 1895, at Los Angeles Shops, and the Los Angeles Division was completely converted to oil by 1901. The Sacramento Division was converted to oil by 1902, and the Salt Lake Division by 1912. By then oil was standard systemwide except on the New Mexico and Rio Grande Divisions

Tender first used with 4332

Tender first used with 4386

where many but not all assigned locomotives used coal until 1950 because of the railroad's 1924 agreement, on purchasing the El Paso & Southwestern, to use coal from the Dawson Fields in New Mexico. Of the 4-8-2's, only the Mt-2's ever burned coal.

Passenger engines built in the early 1900s had tenders equipped with vestibules, whether rectangular, cylindrical, or semicylindrical. The vestibules, equipped with buffers, were supposed to help stabilize the first car of the train. The only SP Mt tenders equipped with vestibules came with the Mt-2's. By the mid-1920s vestibules, or at least their buffers, had been removed from most SP tenders, including those on the Mt-2 tenders.

Some locomotives in the late 1920s and early 1930s were lettered and numbered with either raised brass or nickel-plated figures. Photos show that Mt Nos. 4300, 4350 and 4390 received the nickel-plated figures as an extra touch. These engines represented the first, the 51st, and the last in the 4300 series. The 4300 didn't have the raised letters originally, but obtained them when it was assigned a 160-C-3 tender in October, 1930. The other two engines were fitted with raised letters when new. Locomotive 4334 had similar raised brass figures in the early 1940s and the 4302 appears to have raised letters on the cab only in a 1932 photo. For the most part the raised figures were removed from Southern Pacific locomotives in the early 1940s, but they persisted on some passenger terminal switchers until the end of steam.

During the steam era the Southern Pacific maintained a 5 x 8-inch card file for their fleet of tenders. This file was started in 1922 in conjunction with the final tender classification system. Each tender had a card. Various kinds of data were recorded on the card such as tender class, tender number, dimensional data, capacities, truck, brake and draft gear type, and ownership (i.e. CP, SP, EP & SW, etc.) Construction date, builder and original locomotive assignment are usually given, as well as former tender numbers under the 1913 classi-

fication system or numbers used by former owners such as the EP & SW. Modifications to the tender with date and shop were usually recorded: extra manholes, piping changes, installation of derailment safety guides, and so on. Examples of these cards were published in an appendix to the book *Pacific – 2472's Family Album*, by K.G. Johnsen; see References (p. 168).

The card also listed in chronological sequence each locomotive to which the tender was assigned, with date and place of assignment. These cards reveal that on the Southern Pacific it was a rare tender that remained with one locomotive for more than a few months or years, at least until about 1940. The 12,000-gallon Vanderbilt tenders were the most frequently reassigned tenders on SP. The 4-8-2's used these tenders extensively and some had many tender assignments over their lifetime. In the twenties and thirties most of the Mt class locomotives averaged about 5 or 6 different tenders each year! Some Mt's had as many as 11 different tenders in one year, which suggests the tenders were changed even at staybolt inspections and boiler washings. Locomotive assignment and operating conditions dictated the size tank used. When an engine went in for a shopping it usually came out with a different tender, even though the different tender might have been the same size and class as it had before. The assignment depended on which tender of the proper size the tank shop had ready at the time the locomotive was due to be placed back into service. This practice became less common in the late 1940s. In late steam days most locomotives kept the same tender for years at a time, sometimes until the end of steam operations.

The tender card also gave the date a car was vacated (taken out of service); tenders were often stored after this date until sold or scrapped by SP. Others eventually went into maintenance of way service as water cars, snowplow tenders, etc. All the Mt-2 160-R-1's became MW cars; the last one, No. 8581 (as MW 3281) was retired in 1975 and is now owned by the 2472 group. ∎

Drawings in this chapter are copyrighted by Arnold Menke and may not be used or copied for commercial purposes without his permission. Drawings of tenders except the 160-C class are all to HO scale, 3.5 mm = 1 foot. All drawings of trucks are to ¼-inch scale. Unless otherwise noted, all photos were furnished by and from the collection of A. S. Menke.

Southern Pacific Tender Classes Used with Mt-class 4-8-2's

Class 120-C-2

Tender numbers	Date built	Builder	Original locomotives
8600-8609	1923	Alco/Schen.	Mt-1, 4300-4309
8610-8643	1923	Baldwin	F-5, 3718-3751
8644-8649	1923	Baldwin	P-10, 2478-2483

Oil capacity: 4,000 gals. (3,790 to marker bar; Weight light: 93,300 lbs.; weight loaded: 224,900 lbs. Water capacity: 12,000 gals.; Journals: $6^{1}/_{2}$ x 12; Cost: $11,913

The Mt-1's kept their 120-C-2's with 4-wheel trucks for a very short time. In March and April, 1924, just after the arrival of the last group of F-5's, 3752-3763, which came with 6-wheel-truck 120-C-3's, the SP swapped their tenders with the 120-C-2's behind 4300-4309. The 6-wheel-truck tenders reduced wheel loading and provided better tracking at passenger train speeds. In the period 1925-1929, however, one of the former P-10 tenders was assigned to Nos. 4326, 4327 and 4341. They were the last Mt's to use a 120-C-2.

The 120-C-2's introduced clasp brakes, a feature that became standard on all future tender orders. The most distinctive feature of these cars was the sideframe casting of the trucks, which had a hump in the frame above each journal. Also, the ends of the side frame curved inward to support the brake shoe hangers. As built, these cars had a single water manhole, but between 1929 and 1941 three more manholes were added. The cost listed above is for the Mt tenders. The Baldwin tanks cost $11,118-11,125.

One tender was saved for display at Yuma, Arizona behind 2-8-0 No. 2521.

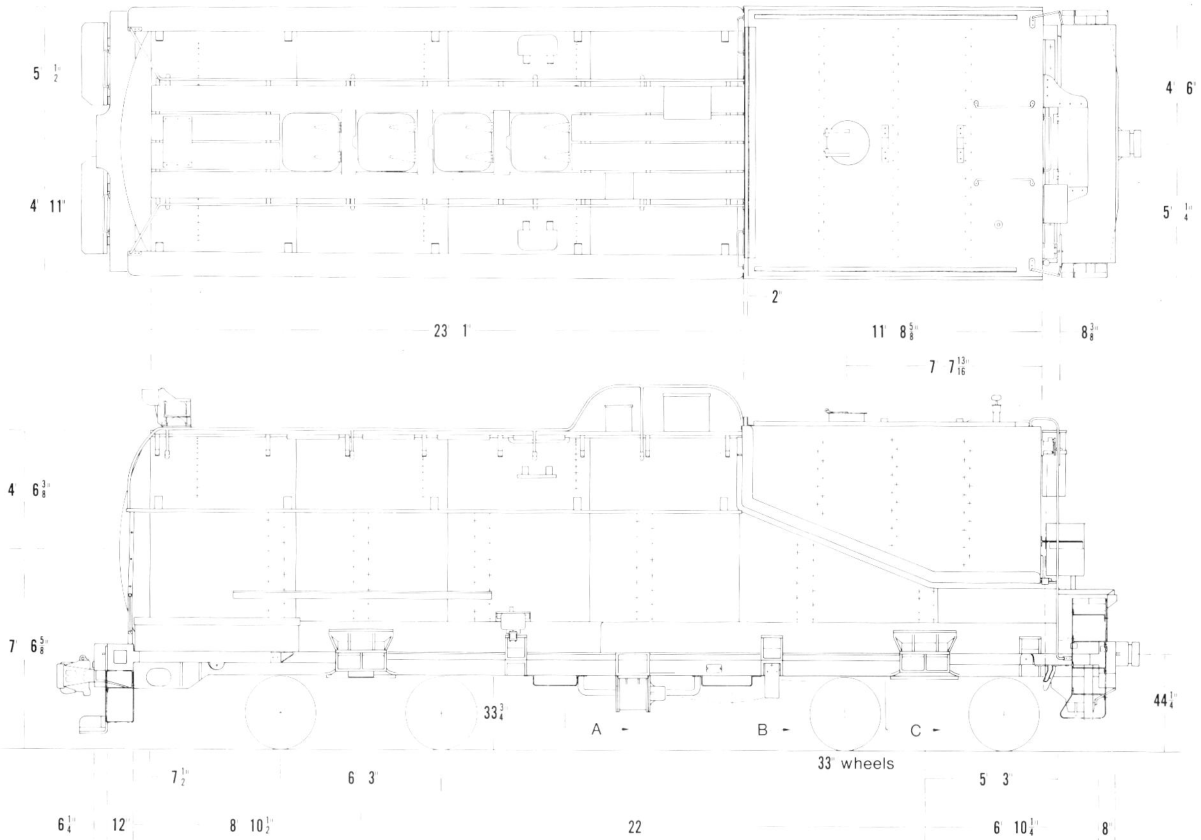

5 $\frac{1}{2}$'

4' 6'

4' 11'

5 $\frac{1}{4}$'

2'

23 1'

11' 8 $\frac{5}{8}$"

8 $\frac{3}{8}$"

7 7 $\frac{13}{16}$"

4' 6 $\frac{3}{8}$"

7' 6 $\frac{5}{8}$"

33 $\frac{3}{4}$"

A ►   B ►   C ►

44 $\frac{1}{4}$"

33' wheels

7 $\frac{1}{2}$'   6 3'   5 3'

6 $\frac{1}{4}$'   12'   8 10 $\frac{1}{2}$'   22'   6' 10 $\frac{1}{4}$'   8'

Front end sill and buffer shown
modified for use with C-9 2521

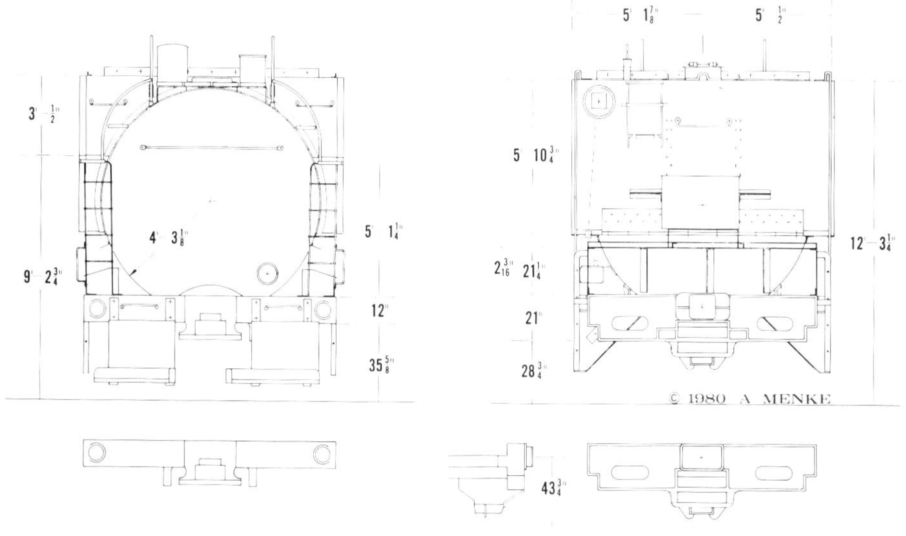

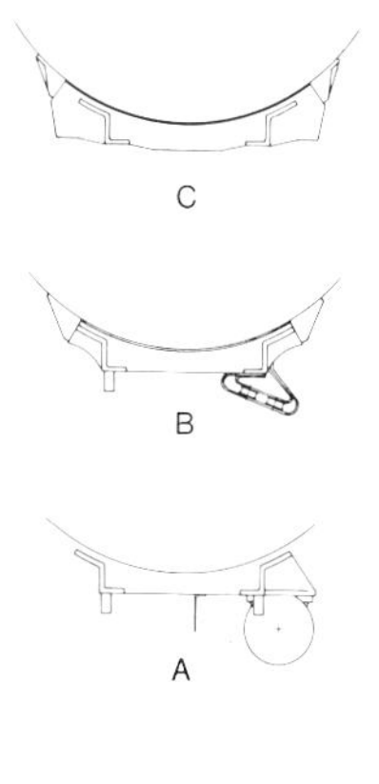

3' $\frac{1}{2}$"

5 1 $\frac{7}{8}$"   5' 1 $\frac{1}{2}$"

5 10 $\frac{3}{4}$"

C

4' 3 $\frac{1}{8}$"   5 1 $\frac{1}{4}$"

12' 3 $\frac{1}{4}$"

9' 2 $\frac{3}{4}$"

2 $\frac{3}{16}$" 21 $\frac{1}{4}$"

B

12'

21'

35 $\frac{5}{8}$"

28 $\frac{3}{4}$"

© 1980 A MENKE

A

43 $\frac{3}{4}$"

Original end sill and buffer configuration

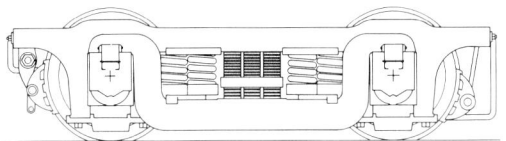

Left – Truck sideframe for 120-C-2, Commonwealth Steel Co. (abbreviated CSC) pattern No. 12822 from 1923. Note that brake rigging is different at each end of the truck.

Class 120-C-3

Tender numbers	Date built	Builder	Original locomotives
8650-8667	1924	Alco/Schen.	Mt-1, 4310-4327
8668-8684	1924	Baldwin	F-5, 3752-3768
8685-8692	1924	Baldwin	P-10, 2484-2491
8693	1925	Baldwin	F-6, 3769

Oil capacity: 4,000 gals. (3,790 to marker bar); Weight light: 110,300 lbs.; weight loaded: 241,900 lbs.
Water capacity: 12,000 gals.; Journals: 6 x 11; Cost: $9,998.

These tenders introduced Commonwealth Steel Company's 6-wheel equalized pedestal trucks to the SP. This type of truck became standard on future orders until the advent of the large rectangular tenders pur-chased in 1937. The 120-C-3's remained in use behind 4-8-2's until the end of steam.

The trucks on these tenders were unique. As built, the outer axles were not fully equalized, and SP modi-

Tie sprinkler

This 120-C-3 tender still has original truck configuration—no coil spring at end. Fresno, Sept. 9, 1954, F.C. Smith photo.

fied the majority of them by adding a coil spring at each end. The two drawings (next page) show the before and after look. Trucks on a few cars such as the one behind 3647 (photo above) remained as built. When new, these trucks had two small round holes in the side frame above each journal. The SP elongated these for better visibility into the interior.

Originally these tenders came with one water man-

hole, but between 1925-1946 the SP added three more on most cars. Most 120-C-3's had tie sprinklers installed in 1924 just after arrival from the factory (see drawing below). Water deflectors were added to the side of the water tank above the rear truck in 1938-1940 to help keep water off the truck journals. Fenders were also added to the truck side frame above each journal for the same purpose. Most tenders had a small Oliver

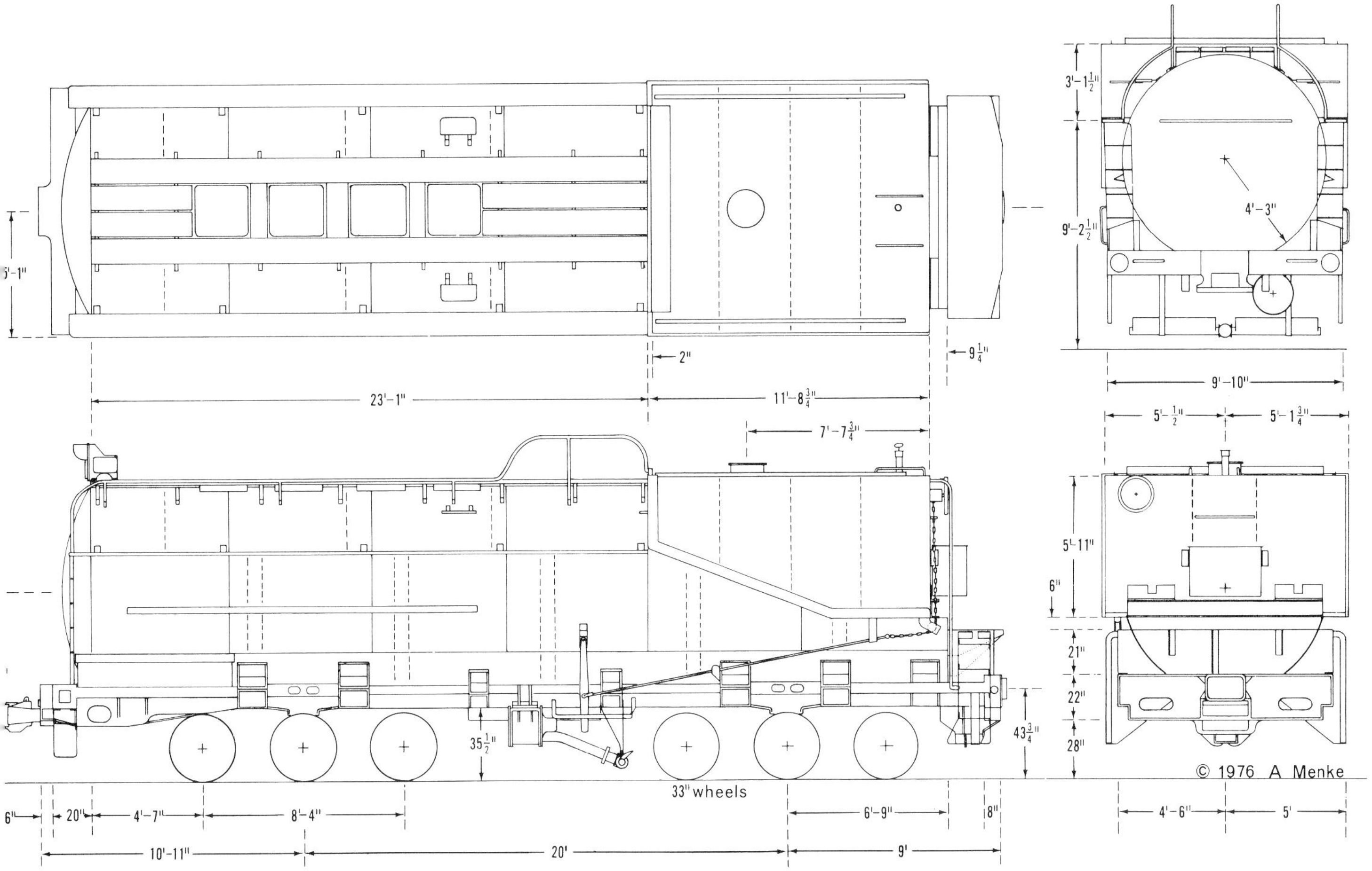

© 1976 A Menke

No. 8658, Oakland, Calif.

backup lamp applied to the rear of the water tank in 1928-30. These were replaced with standard locomotive headlights mounted on the tender deck between the late 1930s and the mid-1940s. Derailment safety guides were applied to the trucks between 1941-46. Some tenders had their journal boxes replaced by the larger, spring-pad lubricators of SP design beginning around 1940. However, most of these were converted back to waste-packed journals in the late 1940s. A few

tenders had air-operated tire cooling piping applied in the early 1940s.

The cost listed above was for the Mt tenders. Those built by Baldwin ranged between $12,899 and $13,280.

Two tenders of this class exist today, both behind P-8's. One, 8666, is with restored 2472, and the other, 8658, is with 2467, formerly displayed in Oakland, but now slated for return to operation. Both are former Mt-1 tenders.

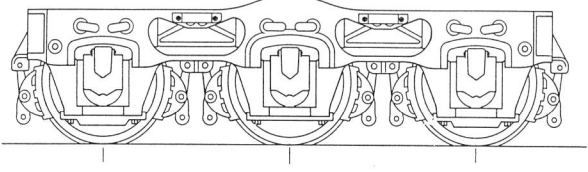 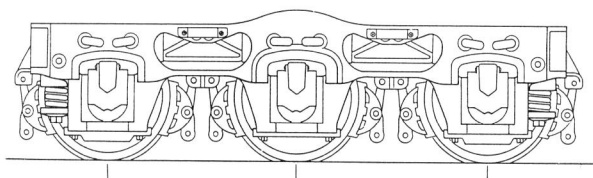

Left – As-built truck (Commonwealth Steel, CSC, pattern 12613). Right – SP modification with added end coil springs.

Class 120-C-4

Tender number	Date built	Builder	Original locomotive
8694	1925	Alco/Schen.	SP-1, 5000

Oil capacity: 4,000 gals. (3,790 to marker bar; Weight light: 113,300 lbs.; weight loaded: 244,900 lbs. Water capacity: 12,000 gals.; Journals: 6 x 11; Cost: $11,262.

This one-of-a-kind tender saw very brief usage behind an Mt. It was removed from 4-10-2 5000 in October 1929, and then assigned to 4326, but was removed in February 1930, and was never again behind a 4-8-2.

This tender introduced the staff-type Miner Ideal Safety handbrake. All future SP tenders came with

these instead of the more traditional brake wheel. The 120-C-4 resembled the 120-C-3, but the top deck was full width just behind the oil tank, with short ladders leading down to the running boards. Also, the 120-C-4 had a more advanced Commonwealth truck and a slightly different cast-steel underframe.

Los Angeles, July 20, 1934, G.M. Best photo

Class 120-C-5

Tender numbers	Date built	Builder	Original locomotives
8695-8709	1925	Alco/Schen.	SP-1, 5001-5015

Oil capacity: 4,690 gals. (4,433 to marker bar); Weight light: 113,300 lbs.; weight loaded: 250,200 lbs.
Water capacity: 12,000 gals.; Journals: 6 x 11; Cost: $11,262.

These tenders were permanently removed from assignments behind 4-10-2's between September 1927 and May 1930. Several subsequently saw service behind 4-8-2's up to the end of steam. When tender 8698 was removed from 5004 it was assigned to 4350 in January, 1929. It stayed with 4350 off and on until mid-1940. Early in their association, this tender had raised, plated "SOUTHERN PACIFIC LINES" lettering on the water tank.

The 120-C-5's came with a larger oil tank than previous 12,000-gallon Vanderbilts, and its shape was unique to this class. They had the same underframe and trucks as on Class 120-C-4. The 120-C-5's had four water manholes, the first new tenders so equipped. On subsequent new tenders, four would be standard. The 120-C-5's were the first SP Vanderbilts to incorporate the Robert V. Anderson patent (#1,512,440, Oct. 21, 1924), which improved the manner in which the slope sheet of the fuel bunker was fastened to the water tank of a Vanderbilt tender. The angle iron that was riveted to the two sections had required complex bending, and riveting was always difficult. Anderson's patent overcame this by making the water tank directly beneath the rear of the fuel bunker vertical instead of curving upward and inward. This eliminated the problem.

Most of these tenders received the same additions and modifications noted under class 120-C-3.

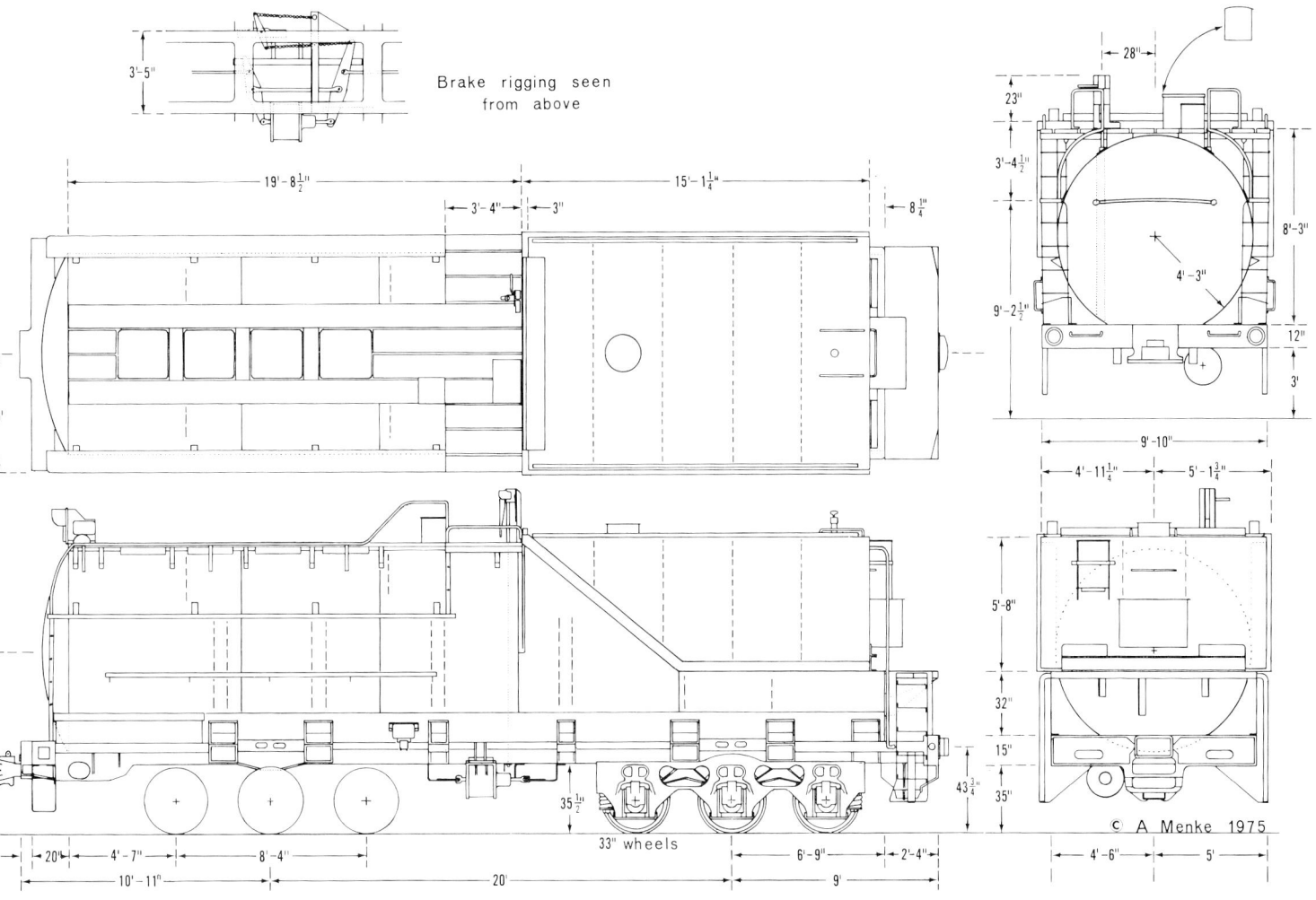

This 120-C-5 tender is behind Mt-5 No. 4369 at Bakersfield on May 31, 1948. R.J. Berry photo.

Class 120-C-6

Tender numbers	Date built	Builder	Original locomotives
8710-8727	1925-26	Sacramento Shops	Mt-3, 4328-4345
8769-8773	1926	Sacramento Shops	Mt-4, 4346-4350

Oil capacity: 4,000 gals. (3,790 to marker bar); Weight light: 110,800 lbs.; weight loaded: 242,400 lbs.
Water capacity: 12,000 gals.; Journals: 6 x 11; Cost: $14,527.

These tenders were built specifically for the Mt's being built at Sacramento. The 120-C-6's were constructed by putting the tanks from disassembled 120-C-1's on new underframes and trucks supplied by Commonwealth Steel Co. Original equipment from the 120-C-1's such as the brake wheel, handrails, etc.

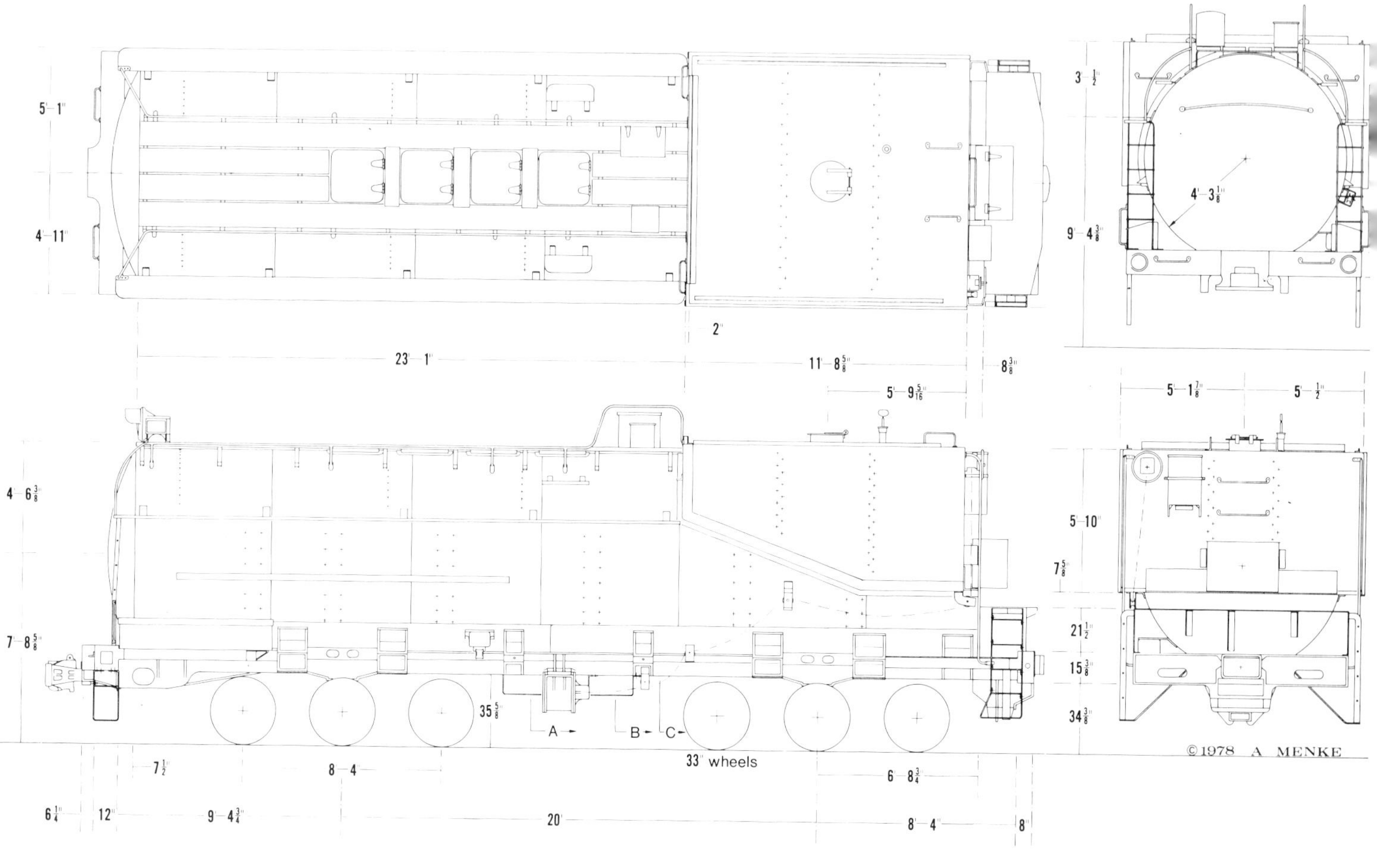

© 1978 A MENKE

120-C-6 had two rivet rows on oil tank, otherwise were similar to 120-C-3's. 4350's tender had raised polished nickel silver lettering.

were retained, although the water manholes were apparently upgraded from one to four at time of construction. The underframe was the same as on Class 120-C-5, as were the trucks on all but the last five cars, those that were built for Mt-4's 4346-4350. These last five tenders had a more modern truck, identical to that used under class 120-C-8. The cost of the cars went up incrementally from the original $14,527. Some of the last ones constructed were listed as $16,258.

These cars look like 120-C-3's but the presence of only two vertical rows of rivets on the oil tank side, the shape of the handrail atop the water tank (behind the oil tank), and the trucks identify them as class 120-C-6. These tenders continued to be used behind 4-8-2's to the end of steam, but they were also assigned to service with 2-10-2's and 4-6-2's.

Class 120-C-8

Tender numbers	Date built	Builder	Original locomotives
8746-8768	1926	Alco/Schen.	SP-2, 5016-5038

Oil capacity: 4,912 gals. (4,692 to marker bar); Weight light: 124,200 lbs.; weight loaded: 264,500 lbs. Water capacity: 12,150 gals.; Journals: 6 x 11; Cost: $11,826.

These tenders represented the last design in the 12,000-gallon series of Vanderbilts on the SP. The oil tank was even larger and the water tank held a trifle more than earlier 120-C's. A spotting feature of these tenders was the horizontal rivet line in the side of the oil bunker. The trucks were the same as used under the last five of the 120-C-6's. These tenders were permanently removed from 4-10-2 assignments between October 1928 and July 1930 and placed behind 2-10-2's, 4-6-2's, and 4300s. A few of them were assigned to Mt's until the end of steam. One car, 8759, was assigned to Mt-2 4388 after its rectangular tender was apparently

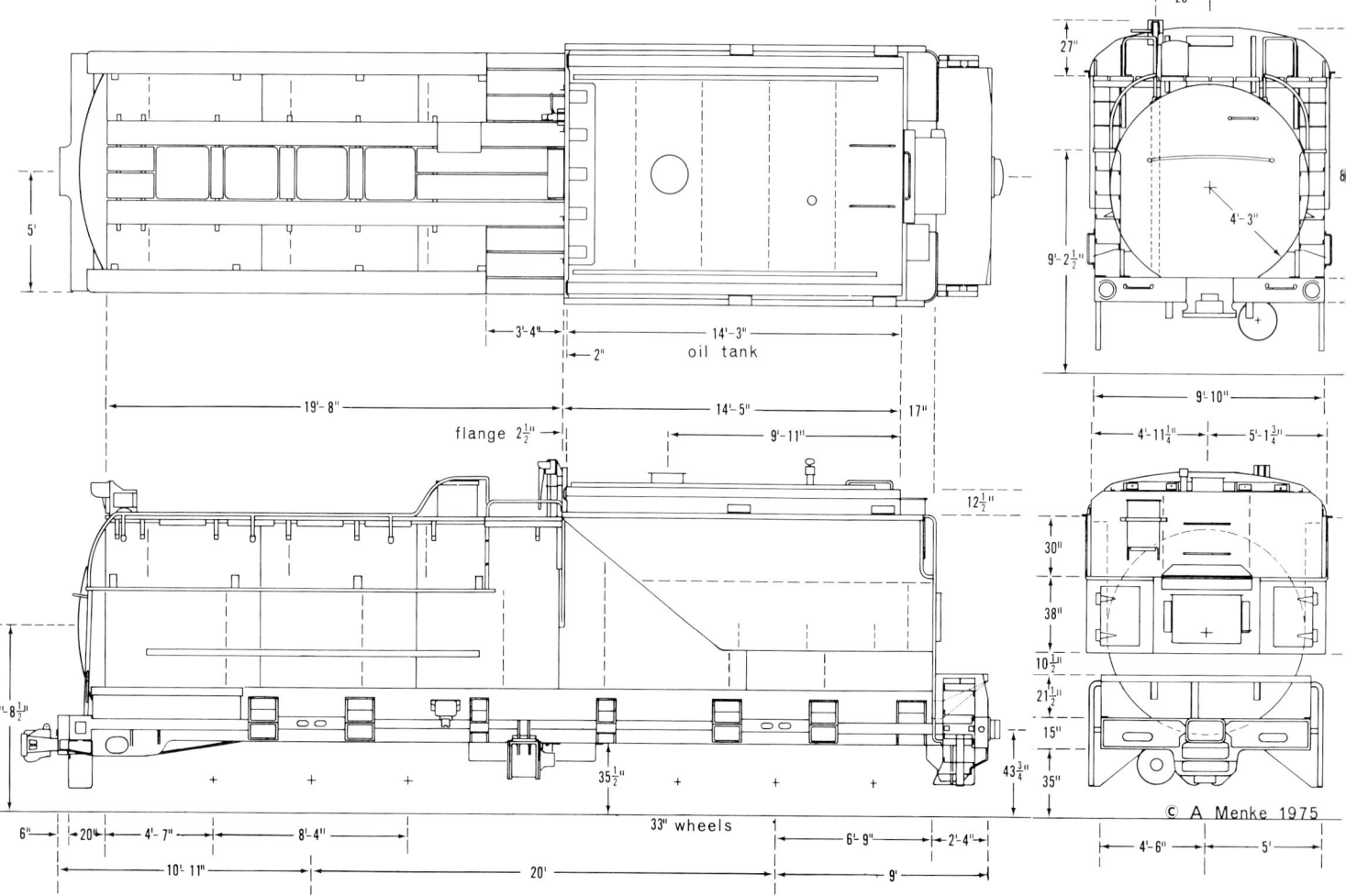

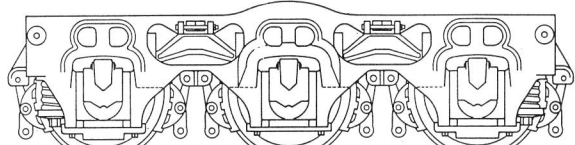

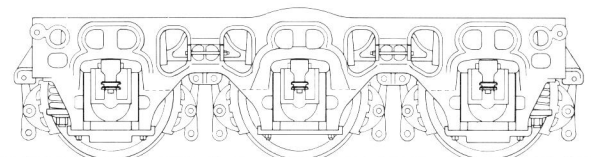

Left – CSC pattern 14707. This truck had 8'-4" wheelbase and was used under 120-C-4 and -5, and 18 of the 120-C-6 tenders.
Right – CSC pattern 16722, used with the last 5 of 120-C-6 and all of 120-C-8 tenders.

Marker light box

Miner hand brake

irreparably damaged in 1934. Except for the assignment of 160-C-3 8876 to 4388 from December 1946 to March 1947, the association of 4388 and 8759 lasted until the engine was retired in 1951.

One of these tenders survives today. It is behind 2479 which was displayed at the Santa Clara County fairgrounds until recently. Now both are undergoing restoration for operation.

Class 123-R-1

Tender numbers	Date built	Builder	Original locomotives
8580-8585	1924	Alco/Brooks	Mt-2, 4385-4390

Coal capacity: 20 tons; Oil capacity: 4,310 gals. (4,100 to marker bar)
Weight light (coal): 115,000 lbs.; weight loaded (coal): 257,500 lbs.
Weight light (oil): 122,500 lbs.; weight loaded (oil): 256,550 lbs.
Water capacity: 12,300 gals.; Journals: 6 x 11; Cost: $13,072.

These tenders, EP&SW class W, Nos. 1-6, were built with coal bunkers, and came equipped with a vestibule and buffer. By 1924 the SP had removed buffers from most or all of their own tenders, and thus the buffers on the 123-R's were an anachronism. It is known that two tenders lost their vestibules and buffers in February, 1926 at El Paso. Presumably the others were so treated around the same time. As coal carriers these tenders were equipped with Standard duPont-Simplex stokers. The Mt-2's were converted to oil burning at Los Angeles and El Paso in 1929-30, when their tenders received oil tanks. In 1932 all 123-R's had

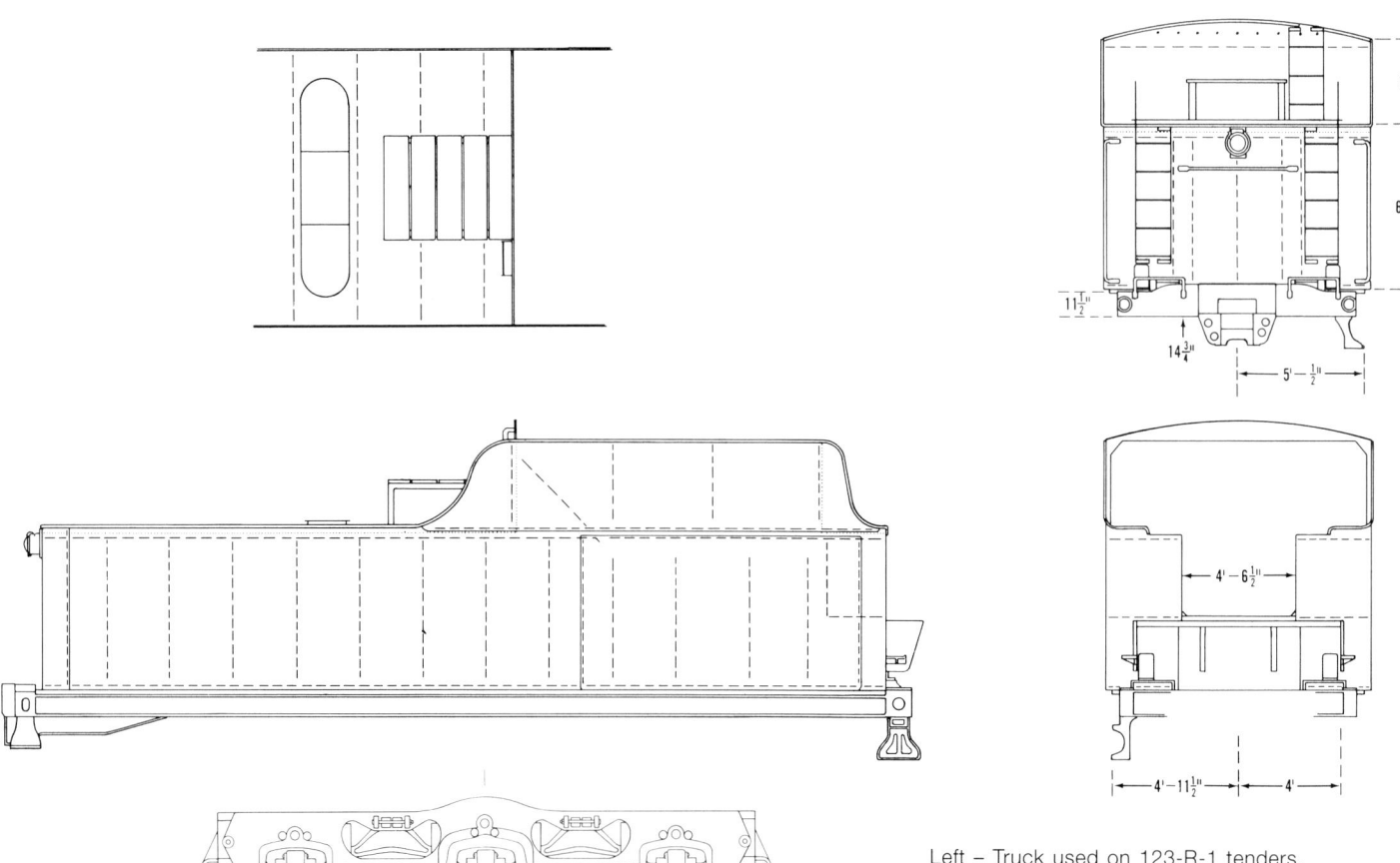

Left – Truck used on 123-R-1 tenders, CSC pattern no. 14308. Wheelbase is 8' 4" with 33" wheels.

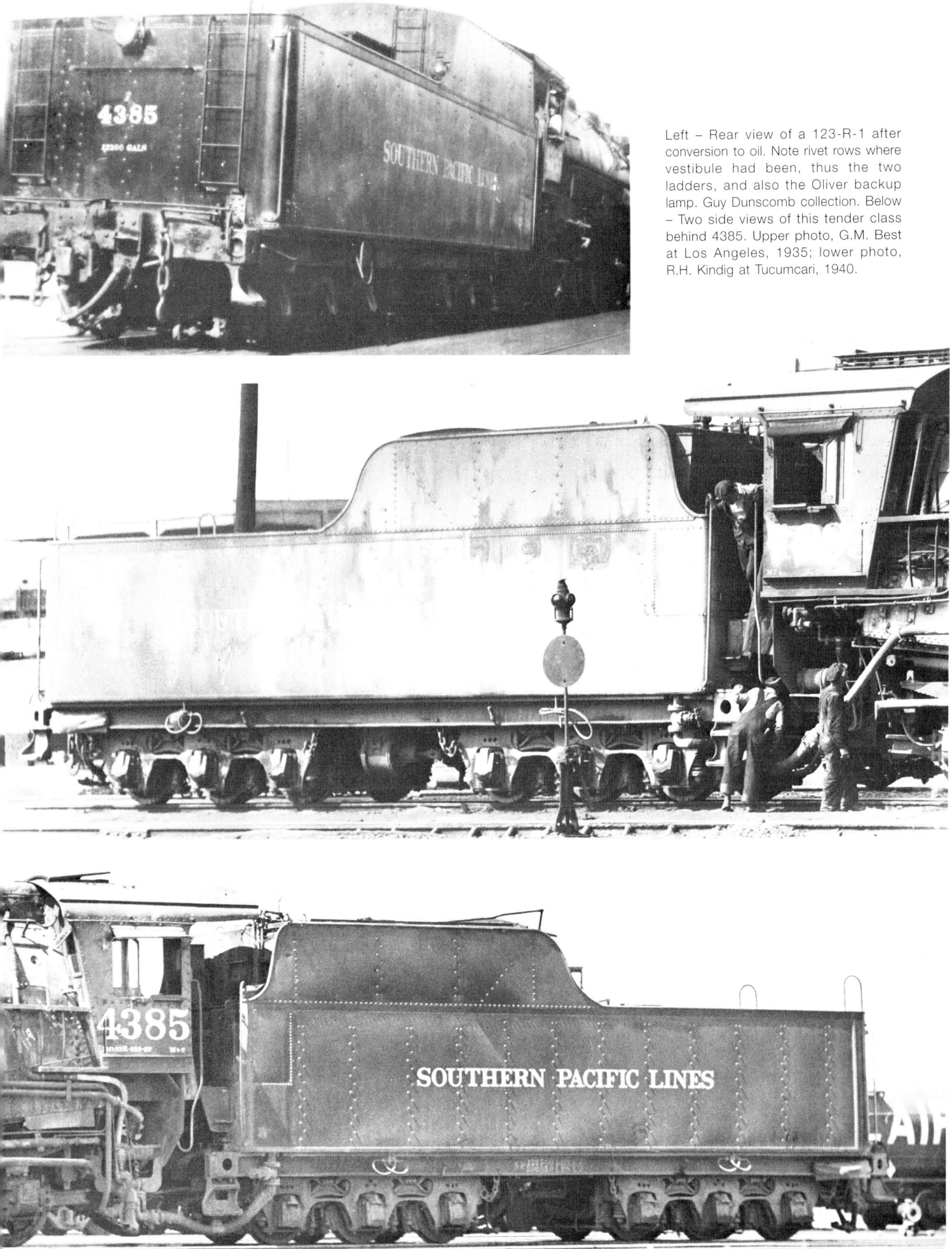

Left – Rear view of a 123-R-1 after conversion to oil. Note rivet rows where vestibule had been, thus the two ladders, and also the Oliver backup lamp. Guy Dunscomb collection. Below – Two side views of this tender class behind 4385. Upper photo, G.M. Best at Los Angeles, 1935; lower photo, R.H. Kindig at Tucumcari, 1940.

Oliver backup lamps applied to the rear tender face.

The Commonwealth trucks under these tenders were unusual; the end of the side frame was angled rather than straight (see drawing, p. 156).

In 1934 tender number 8584 disappeared from the roster and presumably was irreparably damaged in some mishap. In March of 1938 the five remaining tenders were reclassified as 121-R-1, apparently reflecting a change in water capacity when converted to oil. The water capacity was then listed as 12,150 gallons, a slight reduction. Apparently all 121-R's received large, flat-bottomed, spring-pad lubricator journal boxes in 1940.

Class 160-R-1

Tender numbers	Date built	Builder	Original locomotives
8580-8583, 8585	1942-43	El Paso Shops	Mt-2, 4385-4387, 4389, 4390

Oil capacity: 4,178 gals. (3,986 to marker bar); Weight light: 129,700 lbs.; weight loaded: 292,300 lbs.
Water capacity: 15,538 gals.; Journals: 6 x 11.

Water capacity of the 121-R-1 tenders was increased by an addition to the top of the water tank. Although nominally classified as 160-R-1, a class designation of 155-R-1 would have more accurately reflected water capacity. The original tender serial numbers were retained.

Derailment safety guides were applied during rebuilding. Water level indicators were applied during

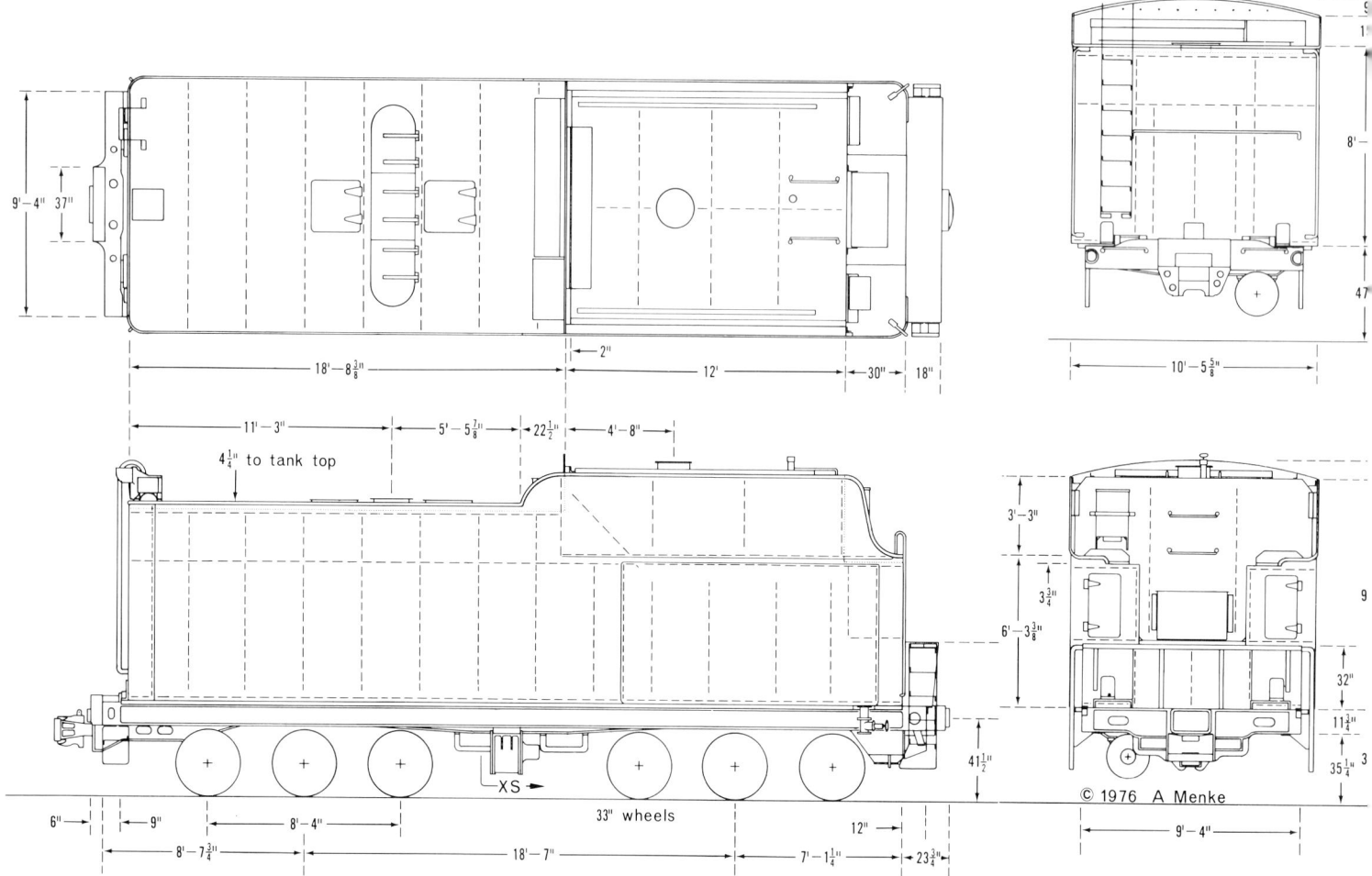

SP MW 3281

1947-48. The spring-pad lubricator journal boxes were replaced with waste-packed boxes in the late 1940s.

These tenders remained with the Mt-2's until the engines were retired. All of them then went into MW service, and one tender, 8581(MW 3281), survives today. It is owned by the 2472 group. The rear ladder from 8581 was removed while the car was still at the scrap yard in Lincoln, California It was subsequently installed on the tender of 4294 at the California State Railroad Museum. The original ladder on the cab-forward tender had been removed when the engine was on display in front of the Sacramento depot.

Class 160-C-1

Tender numbers	Date built	Builder	Original locomotives
8779-8786	1927	Sacramento Shops	Mt-4, 4351-4358
8787-8796	1927	Alco/Schen.	SP-3, 5039-5048

Oil capacity: 4,912 gals. (4,692 to marker bar); Weight light: 119,000 lbs.; weight loaded: 292,700 lbs. Water capacity: 16,152 gals.; Journals: 6 x 11; Cost, $16,239-17,200.

These tenders introduced one-piece Commonwealth cast steel water-bottom frames, and the use of 36-inch diameter wheels. Both features became standard on all future new SP tenders. The frame itself formed the bottom of the water tank, and the tank sides were riveted to it and also welded. Although the sides of the tender had the contour of a cylinder, the top and bottom of the tank were flat. Thus these cars were sometimes described as semicylindrical, though they were simply very large Vanderbilt tenders. In fact they were covered by the Anderson patent (described under Class 120-C-5), and royalties were paid.

By 1930, the SP would own 147 tenders built to the 160-C design, that were segregated into four classes. The trucks used on all of these tenders had a longer wheelbase (8'-10") than those used under the 120-C classes. Over the years many 160-C-1's were interchanged between 4-8-2's and 4-10-2's.

The Sacramento-built 160-C-1's differed from those that came with the 4-10-2's. The front deck was about a foot lower, as seen in the front end photo below. On the Schenectady-built cars the deck was level with the bottom of the space below the sand box. Most (perhaps all) of the Mt-4 tenders had their front decks

Left – The front view of a 160-C-1 shows its tapered front sill. All 160-C-1's and some -2's had this sill, but other -2's and all -3's and -4's had a squared-off sill. Right – The original appearance of the tender rear face is shown.

raised to the same position eventually. Another feature of the 160-C-1's was the tapered front end sill, also visible in the photograph on p. 160. As built, the rear ladders on these tenders ended at the top of the water tank, as seen in the builder shot of the end of 4352's tender. In 1937-38 the right-hand ladder was extended above the top of the water tank to provide a safer handhold. Oliver backup lamps were applied to the rear end of the tenders between 1928 and the early 1930s, but locomotive headlights eventually replaced them. In general, these cars received the same modifications and appliances noted under Class 120-C-3.

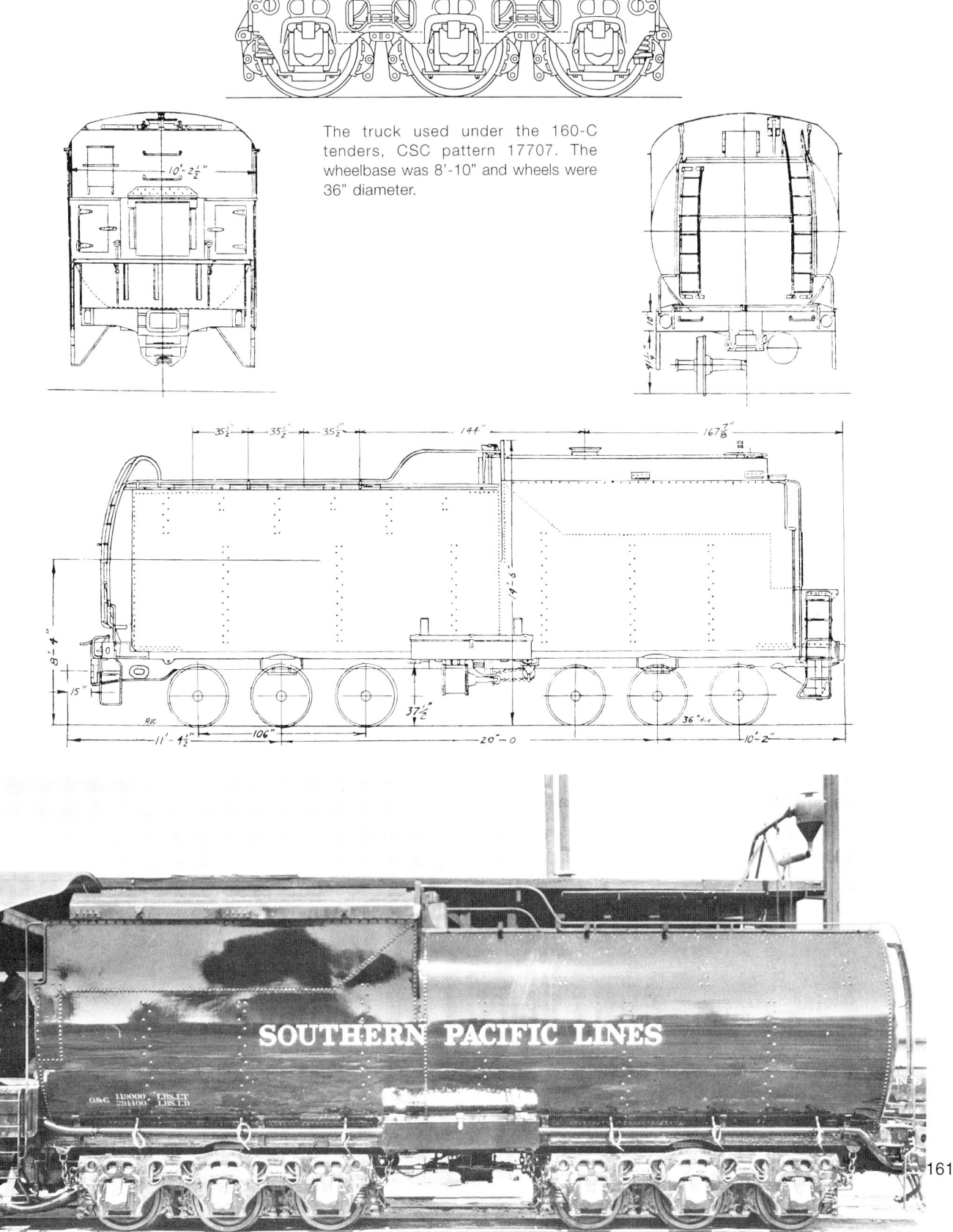

The truck used under the 160-C tenders, CSC pattern 17707. The wheelbase was 8'-10" and wheels were 36" diameter.

SOUTHERN PACIFIC LINES

Class 160-C-2

Tender numbers	Date built	Builder	Original locomotives
8797-8804	1928-29	Sacramento Shops	Mt-4, 4359-4366
8805-8814	1928-29	Sacramento Shops	extras for 4-10-2's
8815-8824	1928	Baldwin	AC-4, 4100-4109
8825-8831	1929-1930	Los Angeles Shops	extras for 4-10-2's
8832-8835	1929	Los Angeles Shops	Mt-5, 4369-4372
8836	1930	Los Angeles Shops	extra for 4-8-2
8837, 8838	1930	Los Angeles Shops	Mt-5, 4373-4374
8839	1930	Los Angeles Shops	extra for 4-10-2
8840, 8841	1930	Los Angeles Shops	Mt-5, 4375-4376
8842-8844	1930	Los Angeles Shops	extras for 4-8-2's
8845-8849	1929	Sacramento Shops	extras for 4-10-2's
8850	1929	Sacramento Shops	Mt-5, 4367
8851-8853	1929	Sacramento Shops	extras for 4-10-2's
8854	1929	Sacramento Shops	Mt-5, 4368
8855-8870	1929	Baldwin	AC-5, 4110-4125

Oil capacity: 4,912 gals. (4,692 to marker bar); Weight light: 119,000 lbs.; weight loaded: 292,700 lbs.

For pressurized tanks: Oil capacity, 4,889 gals. (4,703 to marker bar); Weight light, 120,200 lbs.;
 Weight loaded, 294,000 lbs.

Water capacity: 16,152 gals.; Journals: 6 x 11; Cost, $15,360 for AC-4 tenders.

This was the largest class of 160-C tenders and the 74 cars in it represented two different versions. The AC tenders had pressurized oil tanks that held slightly less fuel, but the cars weighed more because of the extra bracing inside the oil tank. The non-AC tenders were just like class 160-C-1. It would have been more logical to put the AC tenders in a separate class. The AC tenders were not used behind other power until some of the cab-forwards were retired in the early 1950s. One AC-4 tender was first assigned to 4358 and then to 4300 between 1953-1956. Over the years other 160-C-2's were swapped between 4-8-2's, 4-10-2's and 2-10-2's. Tender 8834 was assigned to 4376 when both were involved in a wreck at Palisade, Nevada on Feb. 26, 1937.

The tenders were not numbered in chronological order; the Los Angeles Shops cars were the last 160-C-2's built, but they were assigned numbers in the middle of the series. Possibly the number blocks were assigned prior to actual construction.

Tenders 8797 to 8824 had the same tapered front end sill found on class 160-C-l, but the sill ends were square on 8825-8870. The next two classes of 160-C's also came with squared-off front end sills. Backup lamps were applied to the rear end of Mt tenders in 1934, but tenders behind AC-4's and SP's received theirs between 1929 and 1938. Apparently most of the Los Angeles Shop tenders had these lamps installed during construction; the same may have been true for the cars built in Sacramento in the latter part of 1929. The AC-5 tenders had backup lamps applied by Baldwin. Locomotive headlights began to replace backup lamps in 1938, but some tenders did not get one until 1945.

Many 160-C-2's received spring-pad lubricator journal boxes between 1938 and 1944, but by the late 1940s they were being replaced with waste-packed boxes. Water deflectors and derailment safety guides were applied to all tenders in the late 1930s and early 1940s. Some tenders received air-operated tire coolers and water tank level indicators.

One tender of Class 160-C-2 survives today. Number 8848 is preserved with engine 5021 at the Pomona Fairgrounds in southern California. This tender never saw service with a 4-8-2.

Views of the deck of the 160-C-2 tender preserved at Pomona. Clearly shown are the braces on the bulkhead behind the oil tank (left) and the details of manhole lids and the semi-circular cut of the end of the deck boards (right).

Class 160-C-3

Tender numbers	Date built	Builder	Original locomotives
8871-8890	1930	Los Angeles Shops	extras for 4-8-2's and 4-10-2's
8891-8915	1930	Baldwin	AC-6, 4126-4150

Oil capacity: 4,912 gals. (4,692 to marker bar); Weight light: 119,000 lbs.; weight loaded: 292,700 lbs.

For pressurized tanks: Oil capacity, 4,889 gals. (4,703 to marker bar); Weight light, 124,100 lbs.;
    Weight loaded, 297,900 lbs.

Water capacity: 16,152 gals.; Journals: 6 x 11.

These tenders were essentially duplicates of the previous two classes, but as with the 160-C-2's, there were two types of cars constructed. The tenders built at Los Angeles Shops were standard 160-C's, but the AC-6 cars had pressurized oil tanks of slightly less capacity. For reasons unknown, the AC tenders also weighed a bit more than those in Class 160-C-2. The pair of handrails on top of the oil tank were much higher on the 160-C-3 and -4's, and were very conspicuous. The very last Vanderbilts purchased by the Southern Pacific were the AC-6 tenders. They were constructed later in 1930 than the cars in the next class, 160-C-4.

The twenty tenders built in Los Angeles were extras for application to 4-10-2's and 4-8-2's, some of which were still using 12,000-gallon Vanderbilts. The 160-C-3's received the same kinds of upgrading noted under previous classes. Many received spring-pad lubricator journal boxes during 1941-44, but some were replaced by waste-packed journals as early as 1947. Some of the AC tenders had electric horns applied in 1949-52. These were mounted on the top deck at the rear and were to be used as a warning signal when backing up.

Class 160-C-4

Tender numbers	Date built	Builder	Original locomotives
8916-8925	1930	Baldwin	GS-1, 4400-4409
8926-8629	1930	Baldwin	GS-1, 700-703 (T&NO)

Oil capacity: 4,912 gals. (4,692 to marker bar); Weight light: 121,300 lbs.; weight loaded: 295,000 lbs.

Water capacity: 16,152 gals.; Journals: 6 x 11.

The 160-C-4's were the heaviest of the standard 160-C's by a little more than a ton for reasons unknown. The 160-C-4's were not the last built of the 160-C's. That honor fell to the 160-C-3 tenders built for Class AC-6 late in 1930.

The GS-1's received larger tenders in April, 1937, rectangular cars assigned to Class 220-R-1. Their original 160-C-4's were then assigned to 4-8-2's exclusively.

Tenders 8926-8929 were originally T&NO tenders 2462-2465, Class 160-C-4. When the T&NO GS-1's were transferred to California in 1952-53, and renumbered into the 4400 series, their tenders were also given Pacific Lines serial numbers. As far as known, these four cars never served behind a 4-8-2.

DATA

SOUTHERN PACIFIC 4-8-2 LOCOMOTIVES   Alco-Schenectady 1923-1924

Mt-1

		Shipped	In service, L.A.		scrapped	
4300	*	10-25-23	12-17-23		8-14-57	Luria-SSF
4301		10-25-23	12-19-23		9-20-55	National Metals-LA
4302		10-27-23	12-19-23	x	6-4-54	Purdy-LA
4303	*	10-27-23	12-21-23	x	4-24-59	National Metals-LA
4304		10-29-23	12-21-23	x	11-22-55	Purdy-LA
4305		10-29-23	12-22-23		4-22-55	Bayshore Shops
4306		10-30-23	12-24-23		2-18-53	Sacto
4307	*	10-30-23	12-26-23		12-21-56	Sacto
4308		10-31-23	12-27-23		9-20-55	National Metals-LA
4309		10-31-23	12-27-23		4-27-55	Sacto
4310		3-19-24	5-6-24	x	7-23-54	Purdy-LA
4311	*	3-19-24	5-5-24		10-19-56	Purdy-SSF
4312	*	3-26-24	5-3-24	x	7-14-59	National Metals-LA
4313		3-26-24	5-3-24	x	9-8-54	Purdy-LA
4314		3-**-24	5-17-24		6-8-53	El Paso Shops
4315		4-22-24	5-31-24		6-23-53	El Paso Shops
4316		4-29-24	5-11-24	x	5-25-55	Purdy-LA
4317		4-22-24	5-12-24		11-13-52	El Paso (Wrecked)
4318		3-25-24	5-9-24		2-24-56	Sacto
4319		3-25-24	5-11-24		6-21-54	Sacto
4320		3-26-24	5-17-24		8-24-54	Purdy-SSF
4321		3-26-24	5-17-24	x	12-10-54	Oakland
4322		3-27-24	5-11-24		5-26-53	Bayshore Shops
4323		3-27-24	5-10-24		4-3-53	Sacto
4324	*	3-29-24	5-17-24	x	2-6-57	Luria-Richmond
4325	*	3-31-24	5-31-24		12-29-54	Purdy-SSF
4326		3-31-24	5-31-24		11-19-54	Sacto
4327		4-5-24	5-31-24	x	12-10-54	Luria-Oakland

**Date unreadable

Built at Sacramento General Shops   In-service and build date the same

Mt-3

		Built		Scrapped	
4328		9-30-25		2-27-53	LA Shops
4329		10-28-25		10-19-53	Brooklyn Shops (Portland)
4330		11-11-25		4-30-56	Sacto
4331		11-25-25		6-11-53	Sacto
4332		12-10-25		1-7-54	LA Shops
4333		12-24-25		8-30-54	Purdy-SSF
4334		1-9-26	x	6-24-55	Luria-LA
4335	*	1-25-26	x	4-24-56	Purdy-LA
4336		2-6-26		9-19-56	Luria-Richmond
4337	*	2-25-26		10-2-56	Purdy-SSF
4338		3-10-26		6-11-53	Sacto
4339		3-24-26		8-11-54	Purdy-LA
4340	*	4-10-26	x	11-26-58	Purdy-LA
4341		4-24-26	x	6-24-55	Luria-LA
4342	*	5-11-26		9-7-59	Luria-SSF
4343		5-22-26	x	4-18-55	Luria-LA
4344		6-5-26		4-7-55	Sacto
4345		6-16-26		11-25-53	Sacto

Mt-4

		Built		Scrapped	
4346		9-14-26	x	5-1-56	Purdy-LA
4347	*	9-30-26		10-20-57	Purdy-SSF
4348		10-26-26		3-9-53	Sacto
4349		11-11-26	x	5-6-55	Luria-LA
4350		11-30-26		4-21-54	Sacto
4351		9-3-27		6-21-54	Sacto
4352		9-22-27	x	7-11-55	Purdy-LA
4353		10-12-27	x	4-3-56	Luria-LA
4354	*	10-25-27		6-28-57	Luria-SSF
4355		11-10-27		1-31-55	Bayshore
4356		11-25-27		2-24-54	Sacto
4357		12-14-27	x	12-29-58	Purdy-LA
4358	*	12-28-27		7-16-59	Luria-SSF
4359		12-12-28		2-24-54	Sacto
4360	*	12-28-28	x	7-14-59	National Metals-LA
4361		1-18-29		12-21-53	El Paso
4362		1-30-29	x	2-5-55	Luria-LA
4363		2-16-29	x	3-4-55	Luria-LA
4364		2-28-29		4-28-53	Bayshore
4365		3-16-29	x	9-10-54	Purdy-LA
4366		3-23-29		6-24-54	Purdy-SSF

Mt-5

	Built		Scrapped	
4367	11-2-29		4-19-61	Eugene
4368	11-20-29		12-8-54	Purdy-SSF
4369	12-6-29		2-24-54	Sacramento
4370	12-20-29		12-21-56	Sacramento
4371	1-11-30	x	1-21-55	Luria-LA
4372	1-25-30	x	11-16-56	Purdy-SSF
4373	* 2-6-30	x	7-14-59	National Metals-LA
4374	2-18-30	x	6-16-55	Calif. Metals-Pittsburg
4375	3-8-30		12-31-53	El Paso
4376	* 3-21-30		7-5-57	Luria-SSF

Mt-2

	Date Shipped	Date In Service	EP&SW#	Date Re # to SP	Date Rblt. Oil	Date Rblt. 28″ Cyl.		Scrapped	
4385	10-3-24	10- -24	410	11-17-24	3-15-30	5-19-42	x	12-26-51	Luria-Sac
4386	10-3-24	10- -24	411	11-20-24	5-8-30	7-28-39		3-10-52	Calif. Metals, SSF
4387	10-6-24	11- -24	412	11-19-24	2-15-30	3-25-42		4-3-53	Sacto
4388	10-6-24	11- -24	413	11-20-24	10-14-29	5-11-40	x	9-12-51	Luria-Oakland
4389	10-8-24	11- -24	414	11-18-24	11-23-29	6-13-39		2-18-53	Sacto
4390	10-8-24	11- -24	415	11-19-24	4-17-30	7-30-40		12-18-51	Hyman-Michaels, SSF

* Boosters removed, 1953-55
x Date sold for scrap, not necessarily when engine moved off property or actually cut up.

All these dates are when title to engine actually changed from S.P. to party indicated. Data from Chief Clerk - Mechanical Department, Master Classification and Assignment List.

SP 4-8-2 Dispositions by Years (In time order within each year)

1951 (3)
4388   4390   4385

1952 (2)
4386   4317

1953 (16)
4306   4389   4328   4348   4323
4387   4364   4322   4314   4331
4338   4315   4329   4345   4361
4375

1954 (20)
4332   4356   4359   4369   4350
4302   4319   4351   4366   4310
4339   4320   4333   4313   4365
4326   4368   4321   4327   4325

1955 (17)
4371   4355   4362   4363   4344
4343   4305   4309   4349   4316
4374   4334   4341   4352   4301
4308   4304

1956 (11)
4318   4353   4335   4330   4346
4336   4337   4311   4372   4307
4370

1957 (5)
4324   4354   4376   4300   4347

1958 (2)
4340   4357

1959 (6)
4303   4312   4360   4373   4358
4342

1961 (1)
4367

Class MT-2

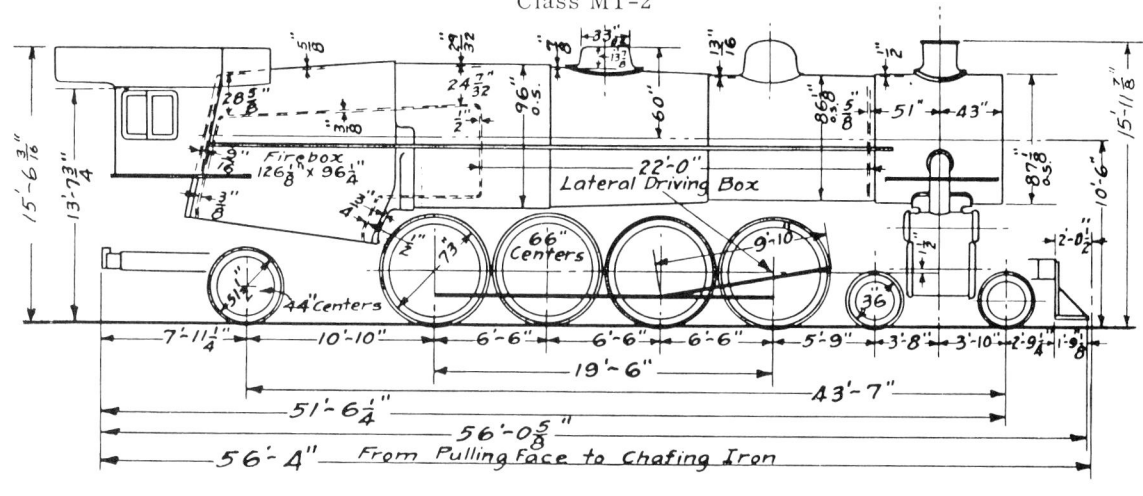

Class MT-3

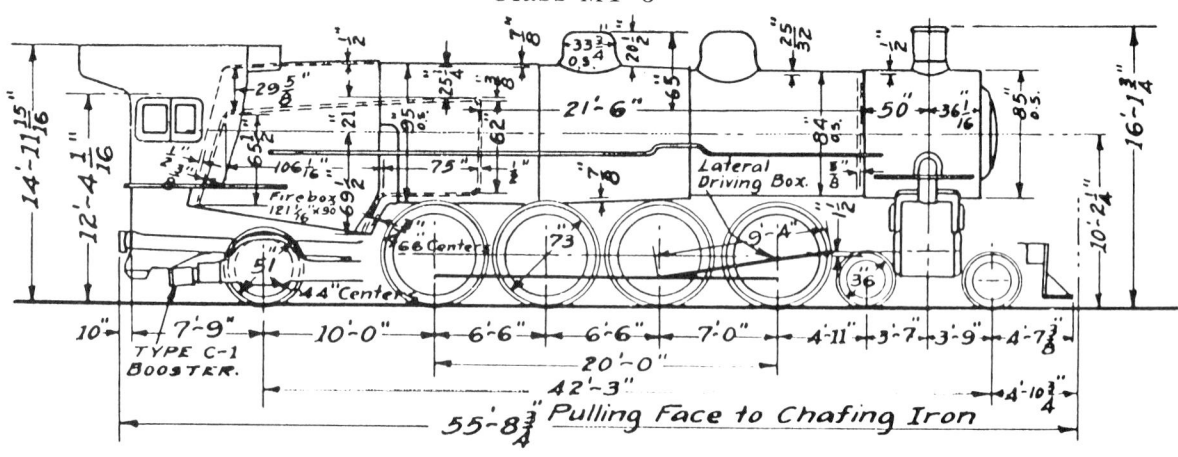

Class MT-4

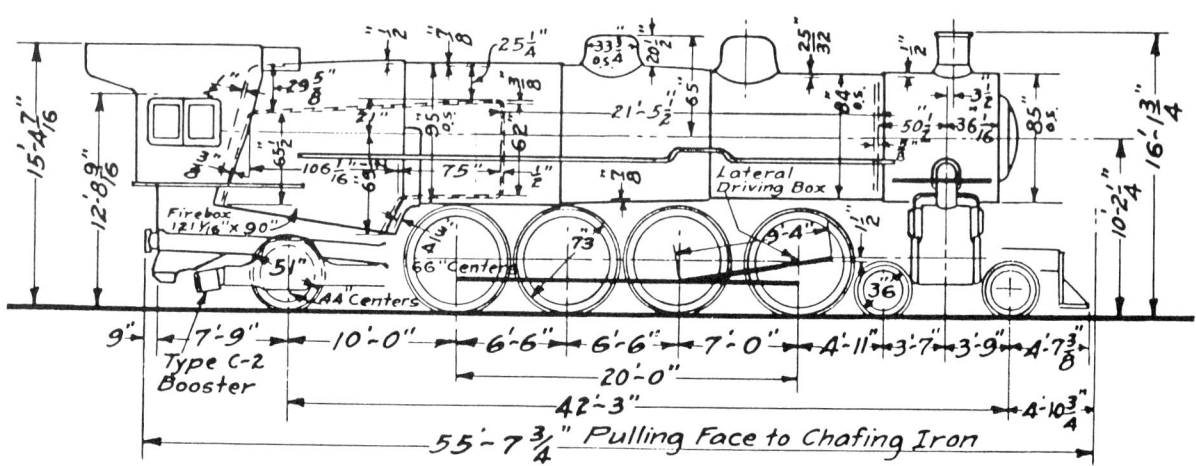

Class MT-5

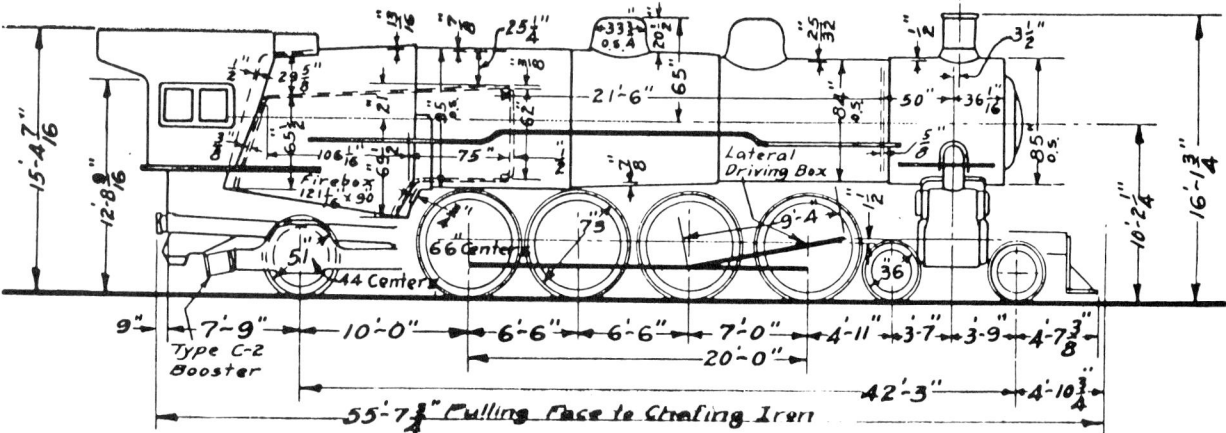

CAB

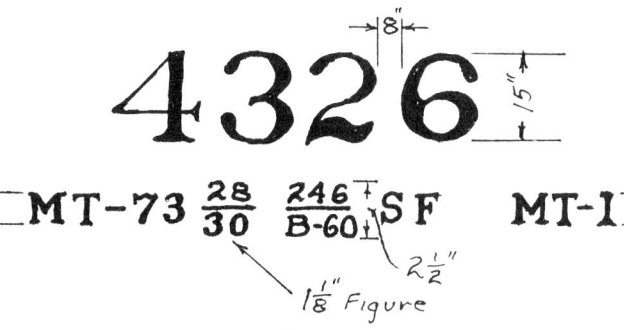

8"
15"
2"

MT-73 $\frac{28}{30}$ $\frac{246}{B-60}$ SF MT-1 $\frac{1}{2}$"

$2\frac{1}{2}$"

$1\frac{1}{8}$" Figure

Back end of cab
Engineers side only

SP — 3"

HEADLIGHT

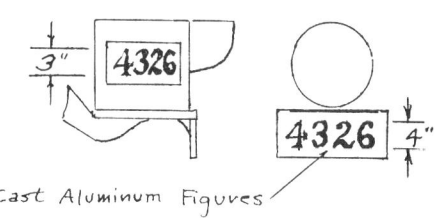

3"

4"

Cast Aluminum Figures

TRAIN INDICATOR

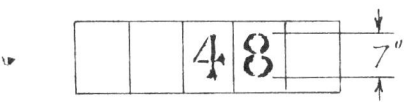

4 8   7"

On this date word "Lines"
to be omitted from Tenders

Revision "A" Relocated "Southern
Pacific" on SC Tenders and added
note for spacing.
Revision "B" Changed height of figures
for Tenders Numbers - at back of Tenders
from 6" to 12".
Revision "C" Showed Location of 12"
numbers on rear of Tenders 235-R-1,
2,3 220-R-1,2,3,4,5,6.
Revision "D" Increased No. on side of
cab of GS with Daylight colors from
10" to 12".
Revision "E" Changed Lettering and
numbering from Aluminum bronze
and White to Synthetic Gray Enamel.
Revision "F" Note to omit Lettering
on Tenders, certain classes.

TENDER DATA

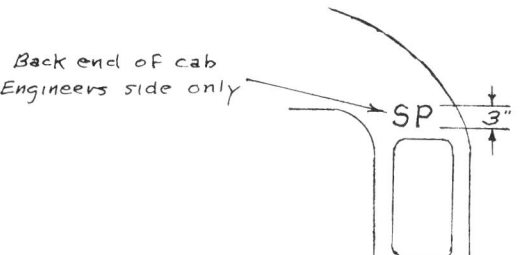

4"
3" SP   000000 LBS LT   3"1"
000000 LBS LD
2"   3"

[Note - Before 1946 Lettering on side of
tender was 9", on rear of tender 6".]

Note - "SOUTHERN PACIFIC" to be omitted
from sides of tender of AC-6 to 12 Classes
assigned to Sacramento, Shasta, Portland and
San Joaquin Divisions, and F' Class on
Shasta Division.

All Lettering
Railroad Roman Characters

All Lettering shall be Gray Synthetic
Enamel. Specification S.P. 198
Color Drift Control Panel No. 151

Size of Lettering to be used on tenders	
Tender Classes	Size of Letters
220-R-1 to 6	20"
222-R-1	20"
235-R-1 to 3	20"
160-C-1 to 4	20"
160-R-1	20"
120-SC-1 to 6	15"
120-R-1,2	15"
120-C-1 to 8	15"
100-C-1 to 7	15"
98-SC-3,5,6	15"
90-R-1 to 7	15"
90-C-1,2	12"
Remaining Classes	9"

SOUTHERN PACIFIC
Common Standard
Lettering and Numbering

June 13, 1946

GROUP 61			
DL 100498	A	B	C
	8-17-46	1-2-47	6-5-47
D	E	F	
8-22-47	10-16-47	12-30-49	

References

Books

Austin, Ed, and Tom Dill, *The Southern Pacific in Oregon*, Pacific Fast Mail, Edmonds, Wash., 1987.

Beebe, Lucius, *The Central Pacific and Southern Pacific Railroads*, Howell-North, Berkeley, Calif., 1963.

Best, Gerald M., and David L. Joslyn, *Locomotives of the Southern Pacific Company*, Bulletin 94, Railway & Locomotive Historical Society, Boston, Mass., 1956.

Church, R.J., *Those Daylight 4-8-4's*, Kratville Publications, Omaha, Nebr., 1976.

Church, Robert J., *Cab-Forward* (Revised Edition), Central Valley Railroad Publications, Wilton, Calif.,1982.

Demoro, Harre W., *Southern Pacific Bay Area Steam*, Chatham Publishing, Burlingame, Calif., 1979.

Diebert, Timothy S., and Joseph A. Strapac, *Steam Locomotive Compendium*, Shade Tree Books, Huntington Beach, Calif., 1987.

Dubin, Arthur D., *More Classic Trains*, Kalmbach Books, Milwaukee, Wis., 1974.

Dunscomb, Guy L., *A Century of Southern Pacific Locomotives* (2nd Ed.), Dunscomb, Modesto, Calif., 1967.

Dunscomb, Guy L., Donald K. Dunscomb and Robert A. Pecotich, *Southern Pacific Steam Pictorial*, Vol. 1, Riverbank, Calif., 1991.

Farrell, Jack, and Mike Pearsall, *The Mountains*, Pacific Fast Mail, Edmonds, Wash., 1977.

Hamman, Rick, *California Central Coast Railways*, Pruett, Boulder, Colo., 1980.

Hofsommer, Don L., *The Southern Pacific, 1901-1985*, Texas A&M Univ. Press, College Station, Tex., 1986.

Huxtable, Nils, *Daylight Reflections*, Steamscenes, W. Vancouver, BC, Canada, 1987.

Johnsen, Kenneth G., *Pacific – 2472's Family Album*, Interurbans Press, Glendale, Calif., 1990.

Johnson, Ralph P., *The Steam Locomotive*, Simmons-Boardman, New York, 1942.

King, Ernest L., and Robert E. Mahaffay, *Main Line*, Doubleday, Garden City, NY, 1948.

Kratville, William W., *Steam, Steel and Limiteds*, Barnhart Press, Omaha, Nebr., 1962.

Kratville, William W., *Golden Rails*, Kratville Publications, Omaha, Nebr., 1965.

Murdock, Dick, *Smoke in the Canyon*, May-Murdock Publications, Ross, Calif., 1986.

Ranks, Harold E., and Wm. W. Kratville, *The Union Pacific Streamliners*, Kratville Publications, Omaha, Nebr., 1974.

Ryan, Dennis, and Joseph Shine, *Southern Pacific Passenger Trains*, Vol. 1: Night Trains of the Coast Route, Four Ways West Publications, La Mirada, Calif., 1986.

Signor, John R., *Rails in the Shadow of Mt. Shasta*, Howell-North, Burbank, Calif., 1982.

Signor, John R., *Tehachapi*, Golden West Books, San Marino, Calif., 1983.

Signor, John R., *Donner Pass*, Golden West Books, San Marino, Calif., 1985.

Signor, John R., *Southern Pacific's Coast Line*, Signature Press, Wilton, Calif., 1995.

Southern Pacific Co., *Diagrams of Locomotives and Tenders*, edited by Richard K. Wright and reprinted by Wright Enterprises, Oakhurst, Calif., 1973.

Southern Pacific Co., *Boiler Repair Manual*, Mechanical Circulars edited by Charles Hoyle, reprinted by Projects 2467/2472, Santa Clara, Calif., 1982.

Thompson, Anthony W., Robert J. Church and Bruce H. Jones, *Pacific Fruit Express*, Central Valley Railroad Publications, Wilton, Calif., 1992.

Westcott, Linn H. (ed.), *Steam Locomotives*, Cyclopedia Vol. 1, Kalmbach Books, Milwaukee, 1960.

Wilson, Neill C., and Frank J. Taylor, *Southern Pacific: The Roaring Story of a Fighting Railroad*, McGraw-Hill, New York, 1952.

Wright, Richard K., *Southern Pacific Daylight* (3rd Ed.),Whistle Stop Publications, Pasadena, Calif., 1977.

Articles and Reports

Babcock, A.H., "An Intensive Analysis of [SP] Locomotive Fuel Use," *Railway Review*, Vol. 72, May 19, 1923, pp. 841-847.

"Handling 11,000 Trains on Time," *Railway Age*, Vol. 87, July 13, 1929, pp. 143, 144.

"Heavy Locomotives for the Southern Pacific," *Railway Mechanical Engineer*, Vol. 95, August 1925, pp. 481-483.

"Improving Locomotive Performance," Part I, *Railway Age*, Vol. 129, Nov. 25, 1950, pp. 23-26; Part II, *ibid.*, Dec. 2, 1950, pp. 64-69.

Lathrop, Gilbert A., "Mile-a-Minute Boxcars," *Railroad*, Vol. 52, No. 3, August 1950, pp. 10-25.

Menke, Arnold S., "Compendium Companion [additions and corrections, Diebert-Strapac]," unpublished ms., 1994-95.

"One-Piece Engine Bed," *Railway Age*, Vol. 81, Sept. 4, 1926, p. 422.

"One-Piece Pilot," *Railway Mechanical and Electrical Engineer*, Vol. 124, April 1950, p. 221.

"Operating a 'Hot-Shot' Division," *Railway Age*, Vol. 116, Feb. 19. 1944, pp. 382-385.

Sims, Don, "Yuma Division," *Trains*, Vol. 17, No. 4, Feb. 1957, pp. 38-51.

"Southern Pacific Company, Pioneers of Western Progress," report, Strassburger & Co., stockbrokers, New York, Aug. 1929.

"Southern Pacific Mountain Type Locomotives," *Locomotive Quarterly*, Vol. 18, No. 1, Fall 1994.

Steinheimer, Richard, "Imperial Valley," *Railroad*, Vol. 62, No. 3, Dec. 1953, pp. 36-57.

Periodical Publications

Locomotive Cyclopedia, Simmons-Boardman, New York.

Southern Pacific Bulletin, Southern Pacific Co., San Francisco.

Poor's Railroad Manual, Poor's, New York; *Moody's Investor's Manual–Railroads*, Moody's, New York.

Index

This book was set in Minion,
a modern typeface designed by Robert Slimbach
for Adobe Systems and issued in 1989.
The name of the face was chosen for its
meaning of "a beloved servant."
The titling face is Franklin Gothic Demi,
a 1980 extension for ITC by Victor Caruso
of the face originally designed by Morris Benton
for American Type Founders and issued in 1905.
Figure captions are Helvetica Neue Light, a 1983 addition
to the family of faces which originated with Max Meidinger's
1956 designs for the Haas foundry of Switzerland.

The entire *Forty-Niner* at Cape Horn. Colfax point helper is 2-8-0 No. 2800, road engine is 4318. Al Phelps photo.